The New H.N.I.C.

The New H.N.I.C.
(HEAD NIGGAS IN CHARGE)

The Death of Civil Rights and the Reign of Hip Hop

TODD BOYD

NEW YORK UNIVERSITY PRESS

New York and London

NEW YORK UNIVERSITY PRESS
New York and London

© 2003 by New York Press

Library of Congress Cataloging-in-Publication Data
Boyd, Todd.
The new H.N.I.C. (head niggas in charge) :
the death of civil rights and the reign of hip hop / Todd boyd.
p. cm.
Includes bibliographical references (p.   ) and index.
ISBN 0-8147-9895-0 (cloth : alk. paper)
1. Hip-hop. 2. African American youth—Social life and customs.
3. African American youth—Social conditions.   4. African American
youth—Political activity.   5. African Americans—Civil rights.
6. African Americans—Intellectual life.   7. African Americans—Social
conditions. 1975–   8. United States—Social life and customs. 1971–
9. United States—Social conditions—1980–   10. United States—Race
relations.   I. Title
E185.86. .B649   2002
305.896'073—dc21   2002009289

New York University Press books are printed on acid-free paper,
and their binding materials are chosen for strength and durability.

Manufactured in the United States of America

10 9 8 7 6 5 4

Contents

For Ed Boyd

the greatest rapper of all time died on March 9th

.

Preface

Game Recognize Game

> Can't worry 'bout/what another nigga think/
> that's liberation/and baby/I want it.
> —Outkast, "Liberation"

What's Beef?

I wish I was a rapper. There are certainly times when I wish I could just drop an album and channel all my ideas, anger, humor, and energy into some music and be done with it. Though I do spit game out of my own platinum mouthpiece like a rapper, I also write books. In doing so, I have always tried to bring a certain energy to my writing; a hip hop energy, if you will.

I am also a competitor and I love the competitive nature of both hip hop and the NBA. I sometimes wish that, for instance, me and my Detroit homie, Michael Eric Dyson, could battle it out, like Jay-Z and Nas, since everyone always wants to compare the two of us. I got mad love for my nigga, Mike D, his skills are without question, but the competitor in me wants to show everybody who really holds it down for Detroit. As far as I'm concerned, we've faced each other only once in head-to-head competition, back in the day, in Philly, at Penn, and I tore his ass up.

For that matter, I'm down to battle any nigga who wants to show their skills. I also want to tell a cat like SC Dub to stop bitin' my shit. Ya know?! Fuck it, that's the kind of competitive spirit that has always defined Black culture and I would love to bring it to this game as well. If we gonna study Black culture, why can't we use it to inform our writing and our performance?

It's all good though. Remember the scene of Isiah Thomas and Kevin McHale shaking hands, after the Pistons had finally put down the mighty Celtics back in the 1988 conference finals. Like any great battle on the basketball court, when the game is over, two real competitors shake hands and walk off the court satisfied and grateful that they have been involved in some serious competition. Game recognize game. Not that it's all competition either, for I am certainly motivated by these same cats to raise my game to a higher level whenever I see or hear them doing their thing.

I write it in this hip hop spirit and hope that you will read it as such. I'm simply trying to keep it real myself. Ultimately, I come in love, not with anger or alienation.

Things Done Changed

It was July 2001 and I was in my city, Detroit, the place where it all started, to celebrate my father's seventy-fifth birthday. This visit just so happened to coincide also with the city's celebration of its three-hundred-year-old birthday. As a part of this birthday celebration, the city was having a big concert in Hart Plaza headlined by the great Stevie Wonder. As it turned out, I would share a first-class plane ride back to Los Angeles with Stevie and his entourage along with another prominent figure, Michigan congressman John Conyers, who happened to be sitting there in first class too. When you count me, Stevie, his crew, and John Conyers, there were more Black people than White in first class. This was a first for me because you can usually count the number of Black people riding on a plane on one hand, not to mention those riding in first class. Only on the way from Detroit, the citadel of Blackness, could this be so.

Birthdays aside and celebrity plane passengers aside, during my stay in Detroit, I got a call from CNN requesting my appearance on the program *Talk Back Live* to discuss the controversy around Jennifer Lopez's use of the word "nigga," the "N word," as it is often referred to now, in a remix of one of her songs, "I'm Real."

As I am riding in the limo to the CNN bureau office in Southfield, Michigan, I get a chance to peer from my window, like Dr. Dre in that famous "Been There, Done That" video and survey the city that taught me so much about the word "nigga" in my formative years. This was a word that I had always heard growing up and I was always fascinated by its multiple meanings. It could be used in love—"my nigga." It could be used in hate—"fuck you, nigger." But most often it was just another word—"nigga please"—considering the ease and comfort conveyed during the numerous times it was uttered.

In a segment in one of my all-time-favorite films, *Superfly* (1972), the main character Priest is in the kitchen of his man Scatter's club and he is trying to get Scatter to set him up with a new dope connect when the word is brilliantly tossed around in all of its different manifestations. Considering the way that Black people have always redefined language, "nigga" becomes an all-purpose word, similar to the way Bernie Mac describes the word "muthafucka" in his routine from *The Original Kings of Comedy* (2000). Anyway, not knowing the other guests on the show that day, I did not know what exactly would be said, but I did know that it would be a rousing discussion because this topic always touches a lot of nerves.

One of the other guests on the show that day turned out to be this cat Speech from the group Arrested Development. I am sure Speech had no idea that I had torn him and his group a new one in my first book, *Am I Black Enough for You?* for their old school retrograde embrace of some Booker T. Washington–style politics. The fact that Arrested Development had not sold a record since '92 had been an endorsement of my position that they were simply another flash in the pan, embraced and rewarded by the mainstream at the expense of hip hop culture itself.

As the show progressed and I got into my groove, I started dropping some knowledge on why people were missing the boat in this instance: they were trying to censor a word and not deal with the real problem underlying that word, which was the continued proliferation of racism in our society.

Frankly, I love the word "nigga." It is my favorite word in the English language because no other word incites more controversy today. To me, hip hop has redefined the word, as it has many others also. No doubt, the word "nigger" has all sorts of negative connotations attached to it. It is rooted in a history that is far from pleasant. "Nigga," though, is something else entirely. The use of this word now, recognizes that language changes over time, and that connotations change as well. Besides, the more you say it, the more you potentially desensitize it. Maybe there will come a time when, after we've drained all of the venom out of this word, we can have a real discussion about racism in this country. As long as it keeps getting swept under the rug, though, forget about it.

There tend to be different reactions to the word, depending on whom you are talking to. Many White people, for instance, have said that they feel there is a double standard when Black people can say it and they cannot. Yet these same people fail to realize that as an African American, you have to accept a racial double standard as an integral part of life. So this idea never held much weight for me.

Speech, on the other hand, like many other Black people, took offense at my words and he began to talk about how many people died over this word and how as a detached academic living in the ivory tower, I had simply lost touch with my Blackness and forgotten about all the history that this word conjures up. This is a cliché of the highest order, and it is one that I have heard before a million times. It is as if, because I am an educated Black man working at a major university, I am somehow immune to the racism that everyday people face.

I guess the LAPD must have forgotten all of my credentials when they pulled me over and put a gun to my head for driving while Black on Tuesday. In spite of my degrees and my accomplishments, I was at that moment reduced to another

Rodney King or worse yet, Kunta Kente. I wonder how long it would have taken them to shoot me if I had tried to explain Derrida's theory of deconstruction to them.

In other words, no matter how much I have done to make something of myself, I'm still a nigger in the eyes of many! No Ph.D., no amount of money or anything else could ever change that. So, if it is inevitable, why not have some fun with it? As Prodigy from Mobb Deep says, "I'm a thorough street nigga for real/just applaud me." Understanding hip hop's constant refiguring of language, I now declare for the world to hear that I am a nigga; an educated, articulate, book writin', filmmakin', media appearin', Jaguar drivin', well-dressed nigga, but a nigga nonetheless!

In the spring of 1997, I became a thirty-two-year-old tenured professor at the number-one film school in the world. I mention this only because at age twenty-one I had flunked out of the University of Florida. Things done changed! Now here I was, tenured and a college professor, of all things. Right around the time my tenure decision came down, my book dropped, and suddenly I was getting calls from major national media outlets all over the country.

Later that summer, thanks to my man Gil Friesen, I was invited to deliver the closing keynote address at the International Design Conference in Aspen. This was, to me, like a coming out party, so I had to represent properly. With a house full of people, I strolled out to the sounds of Miles Davis and tried to put it down the way Miles always did. I felt so good up there, walking the stage, pontificating, talkin' shit, you know, doin' me!

When the lecture was over, I knew I had rocked the house and this was a gratifying feeling, like having just scored thirty- eight points and grabbed sixteen rebounds in the deciding game of the NBA finals. Ron Meyer, the head of Universal Pictures had been scheduled to be interviewed after my talk. He came up, showed love, and said how much he enjoyed my words. He also said that he thought the organizers had set him up because he felt that coming up after me was like getting onstage after Marvin Gaye had just finished performing. I certainly appreciated the compliment and loved the reference to Marvin's show-stopping skills. Life was good and Dr. Boyd was on top of the world, at least momentarily.

When I returned to the University of Southern California that fall, it was obvious things had changed and would continue to change and not always for the better either. As the media appearances increased, the popularity of my classes began to take off, and overall, the culture of Dr. Boyd had begun to take hold. I could sense a different air now filling the rooms I walked into. It was like that old Richard Pryor joke, when he talked about people sitting in the barbershop with the almanac, waiting for somebody to make a mistake.

By the end of the year my former student Rick Famuyiwa and I had successfully sold the script for our first movie, *The Wood,* to MTV Films. This was an exciting moment, considering that Rick had been in the first class I taught at SC back in 1992 and that he had gone on to rousing success with his short film *Blacktop Lingo,* which had been accepted into the 1996 Sundance Film Festival. Rick was to me like the first great player to leave my program and then do well. I was able to give him what I had myself never experienced while in college or graduate school, a Black mentor. Rick and I had gone from professor/student to business partners and, even more important, we were now friends, or as Outkast would say, "[B]rothas from another mother/kinda like Mel Gibson and Danny Glover. . . ." We had tried unsuccessfully through 1996 to sell scripts and kept getting rejected, so to finally sell one was gratifying for many reasons.

By the time production started on the movie in 1998, the haters had grown in substance and stature. Considering how difficult it is to get a movie made in Hollywood and, more so, how hard it is to get a Black movie made, the spotlight was on me. I was after all a professor, not a scriptwriter or producer. The jealousy and envy increased. I was a marked man.

That next summer when the film was released was the most bittersweet moment in my life. The film opened July 16, 1999, and finished the first weekend at number six in box office revenue. Amazing, considering that Tom Cruise and *Eyes Wide Shut* opened the same weekend, along with *The Blair Witch Project*, which turned out to be the highest-grossing independent film of all time. Mind you, *Star Wars: The Phantom Menace* had come out earlier that summer also. We were in good company, but we held our own and went on to become one of the most profitable movies of that year, considering the amount of money it took to produce the film and its huge returns. We had a critically acclaimed hit movie to be proud of.

Many people, though, acted like the movie had never been made. They either ignored it or found some way to minimize it. I am a professor in the film school now, who had written books and now had made a film, and it was almost like I was just another nigger sweeping the floor. I am not saying that I should have been made president for this, but, in my mind, it was significant and considering the circumstances, it was something to be recognized.

Yet, it did not stop here. Many other people, including Black people, whom I encounter throughout my daily life, were also on my ass about this or that. I remember getting a letter from a casting director named Ruben Cannon after I had written a piece on Spike Lee for the *Los Angeles Times*. Cannon accused me of being "pimped" by the *LA Times* and questioned my Blackness, simply because I chose to critically engage his boy, Spike.

I later ran into Spike himself at a Lakers game. He had dissed me in a magazine article and was going around bad mouthin' me during some of his college lectures. When I spotted him at the game, I thought I would see if he had the nerve to say the same shit to my face. See, Spike had become this unmovable object because he knew he could criticize White people who disagreed with him as racist and then turn around and criticize Black people who did not agree with him as Uncle Toms. So I was going to give him a chance to tell me in person.

I told him not to let my Ph.D. fool him and went on to tell him that we could "settle this like we got some class or we can get into some gangsta shit." Of course, he had a lot to say about my being an Uncle Tom and then he tried to, as we used to say, "loud talk" me. He ended up running off into the rain like a little schoolgirl when he realized that I was the wrong nigga to fuck wit!

I can also remember one of the actors from *The Wood*, Richard T. Jones, confronting me one day on the set of the movie and inquiring why I was drinking espresso. He said, "You Hollywood niggas kill me. You can't drink regular coffee no mo', you got to drink expresso." Sorry, I guess I was supposed to be drinking Folgers?

Over the course of time, I would be hated on at UCLA when I talked about the corrupting commercial influence of Babyface's music; at Stanford when I said that I was indeed a real nigga; and at NYU when at a conference on Jon Hoberman's racist diatribe *Darwin's Athletes* I concluded my remarks by saying simply, "Fuck Jon Hoberman!" I was moderating another panel during the Los Angeles Times Festival of Books and critiquing John Entine, the author of another racist-ass book, *Taboo*, about the physical superiority of Black athletes, when at a certain heated point in the discussion, the security guards came up to shut down the panel. This was an intellectual discussion, mind you, but I guess a Black man cannot do his job with any passion, so somehow, because I raised my voice, it was like Mike Tyson was in the room? The panel was later shown on C-SPAN and it prompted a number of hate e-mails to be sent in my direction, one of which proudly declared that if I ever came to Texas that the cowardly anonymous author would show me how they treat "niggers with big mouths" down in George W. Bush country.

The point of all this is to say that I was getting it from all sides. Many White people were hatin' because they wanted to keep a young nigga in his place, and Black people were hatin' because I was independent of their party-line bullshit. Like Biggie said, "I only got beef with those that violate me/I shall annihilate thee."

In other words, Speech's point about my being detached and stashed away in the ivory tower was about as bogus as a three- dollar bill. No, for me, shit is real in the field, and it has always been and I can't imagine its being any other way; so, bring it on!

During this time I found one of the few places where I could retreat was hip hop. I have always been into hip hop and always thought it to be a poetic sound-track to contemporary Black life. It seemed the more I accomplished, the more peo-ple wanted to hold me back. So I could identify with the struggles that rappers have so eloquently discussed over time. I certainly understood Biggie and Puffy when they talked about having mo' money and that bringing with it mo' problems.

I really got into Jay-Z's music during this time. His matter-of-fact treatment of the life and the world around him spoke volumes to me. He talked about the hard times, celebrated his wealth, elaborated on his success in spite of some seem-ingly insurmountable odds, and did so in ways that no one was doing.

One of my many favorite lines though was when he said, "[W]hile you thumb through The Source/I read The Robb Report," here contrasting the hip hop 'zine *The Source* against the bible for the true playa's lifestyle, *The Robb Report,* one of the few places where you might find, among other things, a used Gulf Stream 5 jet for sale.

I felt Jay-Z when he talked about living the hard-knock life. I also felt him when he stood in front of that Black Bentley Azure dressed in all Black vine, on the cover of *The Hard Knock Life* album. I again felt him when he said, "Niggas test you when your gun go warm," meaning that the minute you think something is taken care of, that's when they start to come after you.

After I purchased my Jaguar, I used to retreat from the madness of all this by occasionally jumping in the car and rollin' all over LA, listening to Jay scream, "[L]ast seen out of state/where I drop my slang/deep in the south/kickin' up much game/rollin' down the highway/switchin' four lanes/screamin' through the sun-roof/money ain't a thang!" For all my detractors I was saying, like Oscar Wilde, "Living well is the best revenge." My job is to make people think. I take this man-date very seriously. Thus my lectures, my writing, my movies, my commentary, my very being all function to make people put their thinking caps on. Like Method Man, "I came to bring the pain/hardcore to the brain!" Therefore I see myself as an agent provocateur, someone endowed with the responsibility of provoking thought. I find that the way to do this is not to say the same thing everyone else is saying but to say what needs to be said, to be real about what comes out of my mouth. In the academy I am a rarity, for so many say what they read in a book but have never lived. To me, you gotta live it, or else it is just rhetoric; don't talk about it, be about it!

> I scored 1.1 on my SAT/and still push a whip/with a right and left AC.
>
> —Redman, "Mi Casa"

Besides, I'm not supposed to be here anyway, right? I scored like 700 on my SAT when I took it back in the day. I flunked out of college at twenty-one. Once I got myself together and got into grad school, I had a professor tell me that he hoped I had left everything in good standing where I had come from, just in case this "experiment" did not work out. The same professor later told me that like most "people from the oral culture" I could speak in an entertaining way, but that, like most other Black people, I could not write.

I get many calls to be on television and provide my commentary on a variety of issues. I want to be seen and heard by as many people as possible, so as to spread my influence. I have never been interested in writing an article for an academic journal that takes three years to come out and will be read only by three other people when it does finally come out. If that's what you want to do, that's your business. Not me.

Then I have Black people who, like Speech, get all bent out of shape because I refuse to recite the Black party line. I received a lot of this type of animosity after I made some comments in the *LA Times* about comedian Steve Harvey and his extremely popular LA radio show. Steve put me on his "hit list," and I began receiving a number of e-mails and phone calls telling me that I was, again, less of a Black man because I choose to criticize my own. Steve and I eventually cooled everything out, but for about ten days, they were ready to revoke my nigga card.

In many instances, Black people have become too complacent, with their heads stuck in the sands of a previous era. Many Black people still think we are in the 1960s, stuck on We Shall Overcome. They cannot imagine themselves, or any other Black people for that matter, doing anything but suffering.

I think the 1960s was a high point for a lot of people and they do not want to leave it behind. Sure, this time was a defining moment. Those struggles paved the way for me, no doubt. But am I beholden to it forever? If so, that is pretty oppressive.

That civil rights shit is heavy and it in no way will work in today's society. You can watch all the reruns of *Eyes on the Prize* that you want, but that day is long gone. With affirmative action now a thing of the past, with race being almost a taboo subject to bring up, and with changing population demographics, the days of civil rights are over. However relevant race remains in our society, we can no longer assume that race is the only factor of identity that defines someone. Race must exist on a continuum that understands that identity is often determined by multiple factors. There is no universal Blackness.

Black people alone do not have enough power or the numbers to assume that they will be able to push forward as they have done in the past. We need to try to align ourselves with Latinos, Asian Americans, progressive White people, and anybody else who is on some new shit, and stop seeing the world through an exclusively Black frame.

I was embarrassed as a Black man that other African Americans did not support the mayoral candidacy of Antonio Villariagosa over James Hahn during the summer 2001 campaign in Los Angeles. All of the prominent LA niggas lined up behind Hahn simply because his father, Kenneth Hahn, had been a "friend of Black people" when he was in office many years ago. Kenneth Hahn was not running for office, his son James was, but hey, if you go to enough Black churches and sit through the service, that alone can get you votes, because people assume you are "comfortable around Black people." Villariagosa represented a progressive political movement that would have vaulted Los Angeles a generation ahead. This city has a majority Latino population and it is well past time that they and their interests are represented properly. The election of Villariagosa would have been a step in the right direction, but the Black gatekeepers were too busy living in the past to recognize the potential of that moment.

The civil rights era has now been reduced to a series of mediated images. It could be Martin Luther King Jr. doing "I Have a Dream" or it could be nameless Black people getting brutalized by Bull Conner. There is a point when these images began to define Black people exclusively. The passive victimized nature of Blackness crops up again and again. It is as though some liberal Whites are comfortable only with these sorts of images, in that the images both confirm the inferiority of Black people and reestablish those Whites' own moral superiority. Many African Americans also feel comfortable with these images because they have become most accustomed to them. I am not talking here about poor Black people, who have many other issues to deal with and some very high hurdles to overcome. I am talking about these middle-class niggas who have become the gatekeepers of Black life.

One of the biggest problems now facing the Black community is the divide between this civil rights generation and the hip hop generation. I grew up in the liminal space between the two. Being too young to claim civil rights as my time and now being somewhat older than most for whom hip hop is their generation, I can access both sides of the equation. But I identify with hip hop.

Though I was four years old when Martin Luther King Jr. was shot, I have no memory of it, other than the one I have constructed via the media since that time. However, I was in the tenth grade when the Sugar Hill Gang dropped "Rappers Delight" in 1979. This was the first example of hip hop moving beyond its New York base. I was a freshman in college when I heard Grand Master Flash and the Furious Five drop "The Message," arguably the most important song in the history of hip hop. It was only a short time after this that I heard Run DMC kick it with "It's Like That."

These moments had more direct influence on my life than Martin Luther King Jr. did. His image and legacy were passed down, given to me by someone else, someone of another generation. Hip hop, though, was all mine. I had experienced it firsthand and have watched it grow from that movement in 1979 to its glorious presence now.

I was there when LL couldn't live without his radio. I was there when LL and Moe Dee were going at it. I was there when Roxanne Shante dropped, when PE dropped, when Ice Cube was Steady Mobbin', when Dre was smoking the Chronic, when they were asking Biggie to give 'em one more chance! And I'm still here now. Like my man Black Thought of the Roots says, "[H]ip hop, you're the love of my life."

In my mind, hip hop has emerged not only to offer a different sense of Blackness but also to alter many of the ways that we understand the function of Blackness, especially as it exists in contemporary popular culture. Much of the misunderstanding that can come about grows out of the fact that we are often still using ideals from a previous era to analyze the situations that emerge today. With hip hop being so vocal, so visible, so empowered through the success that the culture has had, this becomes the dominant mode of address and the primary way in which we can possibly start to make sense of how Blackness functions in the present.

Hip hop has now become a force that operates on a global scale. Having started in the postindustrial rubble of the South Bronx and then moved through America and into the global cultural economy, hip hop has become a form of expression that maintains these roots but also can be made specific to the culture appropriating it. Hip hop, then, is internationally known, nationally recognized, and locally accepted. It has moved from Frisco to Maine, and then on to Spain, from the state's capital to the nation's capital, from the Pineapple to the Big Apple. Hip hop is worldwide.

Hip hop has rejected and now replaced the pious, sanctimonious nature of civil rights as the defining moment of Blackness. In turn, it offers new ways of seeing and understanding what it means to be Black at this pivotal time in history. If more people would actually listen to the music and attempt to understand the culture, then, we would all be better off. Hip hop is not going anywhere. It will only get stronger, better, and faster, like the Six Million Dollar Man, Colonel Steve Austin.

Like hip hop, Dr. Boyd is not going away. My interests have never been solely confined to academia. I saw this as a good base, but I have always wanted to reach the largest number of people possible. In no way do I see this attempt at broad visibility to be at the cost of academic rigor. If anything, I view it as a challenge to speak a language that can be appreciated by those both in and out of the academy.

Some may find my use of language, my style, my "steez," to be problematic, even inappropriate. Others may find it empowering. I am simply trying to suggest that life for me is often similar to the life of a hip hop artist, relative, of course, to the specific circumstances we inhabit. I do what I do and I say what I say because I believe it. There are a lot of professors, writers, and cultural critics who simply talk about it. I live it!

This is my mission, my calling in life, to prompt careful critical thought about so many of the things that happen around us, "irregardless," as the brothas say, of the whims and dictates of the academy, the marketplace, or the public.

Like Mos Def said, "[S]peech is my hammer/bang the world into shape/now let it fall/huh!"

The Notorious D.O.C.
LA, Baby!
05•02

Introduction

Who We Be: Introducin' the New H.N.I.C.

We invite you to somethin' epic. Where we hustle out of a sense of hope-lessness, sort of a desperation. Through that desperation, we 'come ad-dicted, sorta like them fiends we accustomed to servin'. Where we feel we have nothin' to lose. So we offer you, well, we offer our lives. What do you bring to the table?

> —Jay-Z, Introduction to "Can I Live?"

Be all the nigga that you are.

> —Benjamin Bratt as Miguel Pinero, *Pinero* (2001)

Back in the Day

Some may remember a popular Coke commercial from the mid 1990s that featured an interesting parallel between two distinct generations of Black people. As the commercial began, an older Black man, sitting back in his chair, listening to Mar-vin Gaye and Tammi Terrell sing their Motown classic "You're All I Need to Get By." This tune was written by the noted husband-and-wife team of Nick Ashford and Valerie Simpson, and it highlights for many, the quintessential Motown sound of the 1960s. The older Black man in the commercial was, of course, enjoying a Coke while listening to this music that seemed to transport him back to fond memories of another time.

The commercial went on to reveal a younger gentleman, the older man's son, in another part of the house, listening to his own choice of music. The thump of the bass from the son's room overpowered the melodic sounds of Marvin and Tammi. The scene went on to reveal that the loud overpowering music being listened to was that of Wu Tang solider Method Man with Mary J. Blige, the proclaimed "queen of hip hop soul" doing their own hip hop version of the same song made famous by Marvin and Tammi many years before.

Of course, the point of connection was Coke, the soft drink that was suggested to link the generations, in spite of the obvious age and musical differences. The fact that the hook of the song said, "[Y]ou're all I need to get by" clearly implied that Coke functioned as some sort of lifeline that sustained both generations in time of need, and here nurtures them in times of relaxation.

My interest here is obviously not in Coke as a product or sign. No. Though the clever commercial directed by that now larger-than-ever "White nigga" Brett Ratner, who has gone on to accumulate unparalleled riches as the director of the Chris Tucker/Jackie Chan franchise *Rush Hour*, did stand out as a compelling endorsement for Coke, the real substance here lies in the way in which two distinct generations of Black people were juxtaposed against each other by virtue of their musical choices.

To me, "'60s Motown," as I like to call it, is very different from "'70s Motown." My Detroit homie and my father's contemporary, Berry Gordy, was quite successful in the 1960s at using the auto industry's assembly-line approach to create what, in essence, became the first "crossover" music, performed by Blacks but primarily consumed by White audiences. This is not to say that '60s Motown had no Black listeners, for it most certainly did, but it is to say that '60s Motown was less about applying to an overtly Black aesthetic or sensibility, and more about creating a somewhat nonthreatening and ultimately diluted product for the primary purpose of attracting White listeners.

One need not search too far for clues of the success of this project, for the Motown that seems most remembered in our society now comes from this particular period. The overwhelming cultural resonance of a film like *The Big Chill* (1984) or the formerly popular CBS television program *Murphy Brown,* among other things, demonstrate the saturation of 60s Motown into the corridors of Whiteness, without question.

As the assembly-line approach began to show signs of strain in the late '60s, Motown in the '70s would become known for the music that I think truly typifies its significance in terms of the culture that it produced. It is during this period that the individual brilliance of both Marvin Gaye and Stevie Wonder stand out as exemplary of what the label had cultivated. Berry Gordy was initially apprehensive about releasing Gaye's now-classic *What's Going On* album because he suspected it was too controversial for listeners who had become accustomed to the cotton candy that the label was known for.

Gordy finally relented after the single and title track of *What's Going On* rapidly moved out of record stores and became a mainstay on radio stations throughout the country, even becoming an anthem of sorts, in its relationship to the anti-Vietnam sentiment that had swept throughout young America at the time. The song and the album would go on to become one of the most important recordings in the history of American music. Gaye's weaving of the personal and the political here set a new standard for defining true artistry in music that will forever be relevant.

During this same time the gentleman formerly known as Steveland Morris, out of Saginaw, Michigan, would release a series of highly personal and deftly experimental albums that spanned the decade of the 1970s like no other artist. These include *Music of My Mind, Talking Book, Innervisions, Fullfillingness First Finale,* and the venerable *Songs on the Key of Life,* all of which helped to alter Motown from a generic factory-produced label to a label that featured artists of true individuality. Yet, many people still lump all of these eras into one larger equation, and by doing so assume that Motown was singular in its approach and in its history.

All of this notwithstanding, the Marvin and Tammi track for the Coke commercial tends to illuminate a safer version of the Motown sound and thus it codes the Black father in the commercial as being tied to a potentially conservative notion of his favorite culture.

The son in the commercial listens to Meth and Mary, with a signature hip hop boomin' bass line that clearly alerts the listener that even though this is a remake of a popular ballad, the song is far from being "soft." This is hip hop, in the purest form. Even the female singer on the track, Mary J. Blige, defies, or at least modifies what we think about Black femininity in the hip hop world. Mary, though widely celebrated as the "Aretha Franklin" of her generation, is known for past exploits of what would otherwise be thought of male-specific behavior. Her penchant for fistfights, heavy drinking and drug use, and overall "hardness" has made her a favorite of both male and female hip hop listeners who see her behavior as "real." I suggest that rumors about Mary's exploits have endeared her to many hardcore male hip hop fans because she willingly rejects what would be thought of as stereotypically passive feminine behavior so as to "go for hers, like a nigga."

There have been numerous hip hop tunes, including collaborations between The Notorious B.I.G/Lil' Kim and Jay-Z/Foxy Brown, that celebrate ghetto women who are "down for whatever" as the epitome of real Black women who, like their men, clearly have no regard for accepted behavior or decorum. So, even though Mary is singing a ballad, no one sees her as a stereotypically vulnerable woman who can be easily taken advantage of by stronger men. No, instead, in hip hop parlance, Mary might kick a man's ass if he comes at her wrong!

The point is that the remake of "I'll Be There For You/You're All I Need" is really more about a woman's loyalty and her willingness to "be down" in light of the perils of drug dealing often faced by young urban Black men than it is about a more traditional romantic love between the two. Therefore the contrast in the commercial between father and son is one of tremendous proportions. The R&B versus hip hop confrontation can be extrapolated to suggest a larger generational difference at work between the Black people who embrace the civil rights–specific music of 1960s Motown and the Black youth who see no need to embrace their fathers' music, culture, or way of seeing the world. In my mind, like the thumpin' bass sound that overpowers the room in the commercial, hip hop is not simply replacing the culture that came before it but truly overwhelming that generation altogether.

One of the most interesting shifts that continues to take place in Black America is one of a generational nature. As I suggested in my first book, *Am I Black Enough for You?* Black male culture has gone from the prevalence of "Race Man" ideology to that of the "New Black Aesthetic" and then has moved squarely into the realm of the "Nigga." Well, it would be easy to suggest that the race man is truly a product of the civil rights era, having been raised at a time when legalized segregation was still a reality that would forever inform his world, even after this legal practice ended. The New Black Aesthetic, the first generation to come up after this period of legalized segregation, is akin to what Mark Anthony Neal now provocatively calls "soul babies," a generation of people who were

> born between the 1963 March on Washington and the *Bakke* case, children of soul, if you will, who came to maturity in the age of Reaganomics and experienced the change from urban industrialism to deindustrialism, from segregation to desegregation, from essential notions of blackness to metanarratives on blackness, without any nostalgic allegiance to the past (back in the days of Harlem, or the thirteenth-century motherland, for that matter) but firmly in the grasp of the existential corners of this brave new world. (3)

Neal is quite persuasive when pointing out the ways in which this "post-soul" generation is in the process of redefining Blackness for a new era and in doing so displacing the way that their elders went about navigating the world placed before them. As a matter of fact, this post-soul generation exists somewhere between the poles of both the race man and the nigga, between the true civil rights generation and between the hip hop generation.

The occupation of this liminal space is transitional, though, somehow loosely connected to both other eras but not really a part of either entirely. It is a space that has proven to be quite instructive in creating some of our most astute moments of cultural representation and social critique, as evidenced by the likes of, say, Chris Rock, whose work I deal with in this book's first chapter, "No Time for Fake Niggas." Yet, my interest here, lies squarely in the generation that emerges after the soul babies, the hip hop generation, like the Niggas of *Am I Black Enough?* the group now poised to rule the Black world.

Old School/New School

In the fall of 1998 the Atlanta-based hip hop group Outkast released their third album, *Aquemini* (pronounced Ah-qim-in-i), to much critical and commercial fanfare. The first single off the album was an upbeat blues-influenced track titled "Rosa Parks." Though the song had little to do with the real historical figure whose now-legendary refusal to give up her seat on that Alabama bus has made her civil rights royalty, it did use her name and imagery to conjure up a ceremonial unseating of other rappers. The hook for the song "Rosa Parks" says, "[A]h ha/huss that fuss/everybody move to the back of the bus/do you want to bump and slump wit us?/we the type of people make the club get crunk."

Outkast are here challenging other rappers to "move to the back of the bus," in other words, invoking the long-held hip hop tradition of the battle rap, instructing their competitors to get out of the way. Using their trademark southern dialect, the group tell others to "huss that fuss," shut up and move, for they, Outkast, are the type of people who "make the club get crunk," in other words, make you get up and jam, with "crunk" here functioning as a sort of past perfect sense of the word "crank."

Other than the clever metaphor of going to the back of the bus and the obvious title, the song has nothing to do with the real Rosa Parks. Nothing. Yet, Parks and her legal counsel decided to file a lawsuit against the group for using her name in vain, as it were, invoking it without permission and for associating this name with "profanity and vulgarity."

The lawsuit is a strong indication of the huge gulf that currently exists between two distinct generations of Black people, almost forty years since the civil rights movement dominated the public consciousness. Rosa Parks represents a generation of people whose struggles for justice and equality have come to dominate any retelling of America in the 1960s. To the extent that America routinely looks to the 1960s as a turning point in the nation's own historical narrative, the civil rights movement will always be an inherent part of that story, and Rosa Parks's dramatic place will continue to be a integral part of the story as well.

Outkast, though, represent a different generation of Black people, and that happens to be the generation most accurately defined by hip hop culture. Some have attempted to call this Generation X or Generation Y, but these mainstream definitions have little to do with Black people because they were most appropriately terms used to understand dominant White youth culture, and, at best, lump Black youth in this flawed equation as an afterthought.

There was something entirely different going on in Black culture in the years following the 1960s, something unique to the struggles of those who remain the only people in America today whose ancestors were bought here against their will. We can never forget that unlike others who may have come to America fleeing religious or political persecution or in search of a better way of life, African Americans came as chattel, as property, for the purpose of building a nation and an economy that was most certainly not intended for them. That being the case, broad pronouncements and generic descriptions do not apply here. We must be distinct and specific in our explanations, for this was and remains a distinct and specific situation.

In the era immediately following the heyday of civil rights, a new culture began to emerge for Black people in America. With many Black people being afforded the opportunity to live middle- class lifestyles and beyond throughout the 1970s, the contours of the debate shifted somewhat. This is not to suggest that racism has disappeared during this time, but it is to suggest that racism has taken on new forms.

One could argue that the civil rights movement was about access and inclusion, but most of all, in my mind, it was about choice. Once the obvious hurdles of discrimination were removed, it became a situation where one could choose to be part of the mainstream or choose to remain on the outside. Of course, it was never this simple.

To succeed in America for any Black person has never been a guarantee. Those who have "made it," though, have had to struggle in many ways, unique to the individual but collective in terms of the overall difficulties faced by Black people attempting to prosper in a society that once considered a Black person to be three-fifths of a person, if that at all. However problematic, the possibility for inclusion is at least elusively there for many, dangling like the red cape that a bullfighter uses to entice an angry bull, or better yet, like a loaded crack pipe in front of a fiendin' crackhead. In other words, the actual probability of this inclusion is certainly harder to gauge than liberal rhetoric might actually suggest. For this reason, there is a profound difference between those who "came up" before the civil rights movement and those who "came up" after.

The civil rights movement has now been enshrined into the public psyche in ways that would be hard to refute. Martin Luther King Jr. is an American icon of the highest order and the media have reminded us in books, movies, songs, and television programs how vital he and his movement were in shaping America. Though many now incorrectly assume that racism stopped when the movement ended, the movement does now assume a prominent place in the lexicon of American social history.

For the Black people who were part of this generation, the movement has given them a story to tell. These individuals constitute Black America's version of the "greatest generation" that Tom Brokaw, Steven Spielberg, and others have so widely celebrated in terms of White America's World War II generation. One could even argue that the civil rights generation has come to stand as something sacred and deified relative to the Black people who actually participated in it or those who were simply a part of it by default. Either way, civil rights occupies a revered place in the culture and mind-set of many people throughout the society.

Yet for future generations of Black people having to live in post–civil rights America, the burden of civil rights can be a bit too much to bear. Having to see and hear about something that you never had a hand in, though something that you are forever indebted to, is, for sure, an uneasy space to occupy. The post–civil rights generation has been told that they would not be here were it not for those who "laid down their life," and then told again, like the words of that famous Stevie Wonder song that they "haven't done nothing" in comparison to those before them. The post–civil rights generation has been both obligated and dissed at the same time.

To the extent that the graphic, even cinematic nature of civil rights is specific to that era, we cannot expect everything to follow suit. Times have changed. We cannot hold the civil rights generation in contempt because its members were not slaves, nor can we hold the post–civil rights generation hostage because its members did not have to eat at segregated lunch counters. We can, however, attempt to understand the generational differences that distinguish the two groups without allowing civil rights to function as the only way to be Black.

. . .

It is healthy, even necessary, for future generations to reconsider the times of their ancestors. As history is fluid, so too should be the people who are defined by this history. In this regard, hip hop is the place where much of this generational anxiety is being worked out. Many people are immediately taken aback because civil rights is assumed to be political and hip hop is thought to be cultural, at best. Yet, in many cases, what was once considered politics has been supplanted by what is now often about a cultural politics.

In the same way that civil rights leaders spoke to the conditions back in the day, hip hop artists now speak to a populace often disillusioned by those considered overtly political in a traditional sense. When a noted civil rights figure like Jesse Jackson, who has often sat on moral and religious high ground, is revealed to have fathered a child out of wedlock, his overall political message tends to carry much less weight. Jackson's "baby mama drama" is, then, no different from that of numerous rappers or Black athletes whose exploits are often used to indicate the supposed immorality of this present generation. When Jackson appears at the 2001 Source Awards and shouts the hip hop phrase "fo shizzle my nizzle" (for sure, my nigga) to the audience before giving a special award to Baltimore Ravens football star Ray Lewis—who himself was on trial for murder only a year before—it is obvious that hip hop has not only overtaken civil rights as the dominant sentiment in modern Black life, it has consumed it.

All this is to say that we have a generation of Black people, now defined by the many strands that emerge most visibly through hip hop culture, who have decided to take what they want from the mainstream, while leaving behind what they do not care to embrace. Civil rights often imposed a certain unspoken code of moral behavior, which suggested that one should "act right" so as not to offend the tastes of dominant White society and so as to speed up one's entrance into the mainstream, while recognizing that only certain Blacks and a certain Black style would be accepted into the corridors of Whiteness. This having been the case, hip hop can now step in and further the pursuit of fame, fortune, and wealth, without giving up the phat farm, as it were. Hip hop could care less what White people have to say. As a matter of fact, hip hop, more accurately wants to provoke White people and "bourgie ass niggas" to say something, while laughing all the way to the bank. This ultimate disregard for the approval of the mainstream is quite liberating, indeed.

Hip hop is concerned on the other hand with being "real," honoring the truth of one's own convictions, while refusing to bend over to accommodate the dictates of the masses. Unlike the previous generation of people who often compromised or made do, in search of something bigger, hip hop sees compromise as false, fake, and bogus, and, as the untimely deaths of many rappers have clearly indicated, they are willing to die for these beliefs.

Recognizing this, Outkast are simply using the name of Rosa Parks as irony. They see no need to honor or celebrate her as much as they see the need to appropriate her name in service of their own mission. The group recognize that the real Rosa Parks disappeared some time ago, yet her lingering image is there for the taking. Parks is a metaphor, a sign, a reference. Hip hop, though, is rooted in a search for the real, and recognizes that the journey for the real, like a search through the remote caves of Afghanistan, is an elusive one, with many detours prompted by various metaphors, signs, and images along the way. One of the biggest misconceptions about hip hop is that it is literal. It may be real, but it is certainly not literal, and there is a difference.

The lawsuit filed by Rosa Parks and her attorneys is a gesture of unsurpassed arrogance and condescension. It is representative of the contempt that many older Black people feel toward their youthful descendants. In return, the hip hop generation says a collective "fuck you," asserting its independence and freedom of self-determination.

There is little if any real dialogue going on between the respective groups here, though. Yet, in spite of the civil rights generation's disapproval, hip hop continues to move forward, undeterred by this brand of generational "playa hatin."

Many White people have now come to accept the Black people of the civil rights generation as an integral part of the American equation, however grudgingly they may have arrived at this conclusion. This is especially true when considering the redefinition of who constitutes allies and enemies in light of September 11.

Even more important is the fact that this hip hop thang has now spread beyond the boundaries of young Black America into White society as well. Not only has it come to influence suburban White youth with its hard urban sensibility, as evidenced in figures like Eminem and Kid Rock, but it has also seeped into places like rural small-town Georgia as represented by a rapper like Bubba Sparkxxx. Race notwithstanding, I would suggest that Eminem and Bubba Sparkxxx have more in common with their Black hip hop homies than they do with Tom Daschle or Trent Lott.

This was not supposed to happen. This was not the way it was intended. No, hip hop, a genre of music once dismissed as mindless noise, has become a social force, having climbed out of the ghetto, having now moved out of the 'hood and spread across the globe, serving notice to all who would take heed that many of these old civil rights paradigms have at best been commodified and at worst have simply passed on.

Although I would never encourage anyone to ignore one's history, I would suggest that you might get a better read of what's going in the world of Black people today by listening to DMX on *It's Dark and Hell Is Hot* than by listening to repeated broadcasts of Martin Luther King speeches.

The first Black people to experience widespread access to a middle-class lifestyle were those who emerged in the decade immediately following the civil rights movement in the 1970s. As Black people began to infiltrate areas of mainstream society off-limits only a few years before, many of them started to find themselves in the unusual positions of authority. The newness of this space might have been somewhat disconcerting at one level, but it was nonetheless welcome. Many soon began to revel in their newfound success and authority. The affirmative action–specific phrase that often jokingly described these people was denoted by the acronym "H.N.I.C.," which stood for "head nigger in charge." The seeming redundancy of the words "head" and "in charge" was needed to imply what a truly unique set of circumstances these were. George Jefferson, for instance, the erstwhile "Black thousandaire" played to perfection by Sherman Hemsley, often used this phrase, H.N.I.C., to describe himself in the popular 70s sitcom *The Jeffersons*.

Well, there is now a new generation of Head Niggas in Charge and they hail from hip hop culture. In the same way that MLK demanded that people be judged not by the "color of their skin, but by the content of their character" hip hop prefers to be "judged by twelve" instead of being "carried by six." The reality of this perceived short life span has ushered in a force unrivaled before in American popular culture and a force that has surpassed previous political exploits.

Hip hop is like an interdisciplinary academic community, combining the fields of sociology, psychology, political science, English, ethnomusicology, economics, American studies, and African American studies, and offering a choice of electives to its subscribers. The weight of all this is what makes hip hop something far beyond music, and far greater than the fashion, language, and ideology that expresses it. Hip hop is an unrivaled social force; it is a way of being. It is a new way of seeing the world and it is a collective movement that has dethroned civil rights and now commands our undivided attention. The people who form the hip hop generation are the New H.N.I.C. and it is their success and failure, their strength and weakness, their highs and lows, that will illuminate the pages of this book.

Change the Game

The Def Jam record label announced sometime in 1999 that it would be releasing two highly anticipated albums by rappers DMX and Jay-Z, respectively, during the last two weeks of the year. The plan was to end the millennium with the number-one record in the country and begin the new millennium the same way. To no one's surprise, Def Jam was successful in its quest. DMX's *And Then There Was X* ended the year at number one, and Jay-Z's *The Life and Times of S. Carter* opened 2000 at the top of the charts.

Although this may seem less than exceptional now, there was a time in the not too distant past when hip hop was thought to be meaningless noise, simply a passing fad, another annoying youthful trend destined to go the way of disco, the betamax, and Rubik's cubes. Over the course of the past twenty years, however, hip hop culture has gone from being a marginal New York subculture to being a phenomenon that not only has saturated mainstream America but also has had a massive impact at a global level.

This move from marginal to mainstream was even highlighted by a recognized cultural barometer, *Time*, which on its February 5, 1999, cover declared America to be a "Hip Hop Nation." Shortly after, hip hop diva Lauryn Hill, who received five Grammy awards at the 1999 ceremony, and who appeared on the cover of that issue of *Time*, quizzically stated after accepting award number five, "[T]his is crazy . . . cause this is hip hop." Her astonishment at receiving such widespread acclaim while being immersed in a culture once deemed insignificant, even by the music industry, is truly a reflection of the arduous road hip hop has traveled since its meager beginnings in the South Bronx some twenty years earlier.

The significance of this moment though is not solely confined to the current popularity of a music genre, or its musicians. The music and the larger culture that surrounds it, hip hop, emerged from a uniquely African American disposition, and like the blues, jazz, and soul before it, give voice to those who tend to occupy the lowest rungs of the American social ladder.

Though the roots of the culture are informed by the African American oral tradition, as well as the lived conditions of poor Black and Latino youth in postindustrial New York, hip hop has been able to expand from this initial base, and has become, in my mind, a dominant generational voice throughout the world, be they gangbangers in South Central Los Angeles, Algerian immigrants in Paris, or blackface Japanese youth bouncing to the phattest track in Tokyo's Roppongi district, not to mention the proverbial suburban White teenagers or rural "rednecks" who also constitute a large segment of hip hop's consumer base.

> Elvis Presley ain't got no soul/John Coltrane is rock and roll/You may dig on
> the Rolling Stones/but they ain't come up wit that style on they own.
>   —Mos Def, "Rock and Roll"

Yes, like rock and roll before it, hip hop too, defines a generation, but rock and roll was initially derivative, an appropriated form of Black music. When this appropriated form of Black music was performed by White artists, it would provide the soundtrack for the baby boom generation; its impact, again, having an almost exclusive effect on mainstream White society. In other words, rock and roll became *White* music, speaking to various segments of the White masses. Though rock would expose a generational shift during a very transitional time in American social history, it never had the same exclusive impact or significance outside the mainstream.

Hip hop has now revolutionized the times precisely because it is music from the margins that has grown up to consume the mainstream. As Jay-Z says, "[W]e brought the suburbs to the 'hood." However, unlike the blues or the rhythm and blues that formed the basis for rock and roll, hip hop did not need to be repackaged in Whiteface for it to be consumed by the masses, and this is a telling commentary on the historical changes that have taken place in America since the 1960s.

In the late twentieth century and early twenty-first century, popular culture and especially music and sports have became cultural sites where a seemingly uncompromised sense of Blackness could be articulated and even turned into a profitable commodity. Many see this commercial nature of hip hop to be another example of the mainstream consuming the margins. It is my assertion that hip hop never went to the mainstream, the mainstream came to hip hop, and this reversal or shift in power relations underlies the cultural concerns that will form the basis of this book. As hip hop pioneer and present-day rap mogul Russell Simmons says in his book *Life and Def,* "I see hip hop culture as the new American mainstream. We don't change for you; you adapt to us" (4).

Hip hop, a music that in its very definition is about existing on the margins, must now confront life in the mainstream. This has, at times, been difficult, similar to the contradictions experienced by many successful rappers themselves, when their present life of luxury conflicts with their ghetto roots. On another level though, hip hop has become a profound expression of something much larger. The generation that emerged in the aftermath of the civil rights movement remains perplexed over whether they will actually try to integrate with mainstream society or whether they will choose to remain isolated in their own existence.

This classic American dilemma over assimilation has been revisited through hip hop. In some ways, like the characters in Lorraine Hansberry's *A Raisin in the Sun*, we find ourselves back at the same place many African Americans were at in the late 1950s/early 1960s: pushing for integration but constantly asking at what cost.

Hip hop, a social movement in and of itself, has been the most visible expression of this societal trepidation in regard to a full embrace of American society. In my mind, this is evocative of Francis Ford Coppola's *Godfather* saga, in which Italian immigrants try to become American citizens; over the course of their journey, we see the toil and strife involved in making this happen. Though African Americans have faced a more difficult fate relative to mainstream social mobility, they have often demonstrated the same struggles in life, and through cultural expression. Hip hop has become the most compelling contemporary articulation of this age-old American question. It is this examination of post–civil rights African Americans and their struggles regarding this dilemma of assimilation, as expressed through hip hop, that again underlies the motivation for this book.

The ideas of integration and assimilation were key to earlier versions of America's historical narrative, be it the assimilation of European immigrants at the turn of the century, like those in *The Godfather*, or the motive for integration that defined Martin Luther King Jr.'s ideology, and that of the civil rights movement. For this reason, Berry Gordy's early efforts at Motown were directly about using popular culture to accelerate, or at least tap into, this ideological sentiment: selling Black culture to mainstream America.

The Black Power movement, by contrast, was generally thwarted by the state at the mass level, but lingering tenets of this ideology have had a massive impact at the grassroots level. A conscious refusal to integrate with mainstream America now characterizes those Black people who willingly exist in their own world. Hip hop is an outgrowth of this Black nationalist sentiment, though it is important to point out that a very hostile racial climate, amplified during the Reagan/Bush era, should not be overlooked.

Both directly and indirectly, Black nationalist ideology created a provocative dilemma for African Americans. It is one thing to produce culture when people are legally barred from existing in the mainstream, but it is something else entirely for people to produce culture when integration appears to be an option and they choose, for whatever the reasons, not to pursue it. Whereas Motown was packaged for mainstream consumption, hip hop was packaged by the sentiments of Black nationalism, and codified in the logo of the hip hop fashion line FUBU, which means, "for us, by us."

The move from margin to mainstream, then, in the case of hip hop, reveals many critical issues along the way, including the shifting definitions of what is considered marginal and mainstream in contemporary American society. This is true, both for the culture creating the music, and the culture that receives it. Terms like "sell out" and "crossover" are then historically specific and seem to be challenged when confronted with the circumstances of the present. Prior to the 1960s, it was impossible to sell out because no one was buying, yet in the age of hip hop, having the means to buy and sell oneself and one's culture suggests a different level of power and agency at play.

Hip hop culture is for all intents and purposes a modern-day social movement that forces us to redefine what we would normally allow as acceptable in this regard. Hip hop transcends the boundaries of culture, race, and history, while being uniquely informed by all three. The move to the mainstream allows for a thorough investigation of the issues that underlie this particular social movement.

Unlike previous eras when politics and ideology produced culture, hip hop stands at the forefront of contemporary culture for it seems to both reflect and produce the politics and ideology of its time. The salient issues that inform hip hop are rooted in the function of identity, emphasizing race, class, and gender distinctions, in contrast to the mainstream.

At some overt level, hip hop has always been about the cultural identity of those who perform the music, and those who constitute its core audience. This concern over identity is generally bounded by two other primary issues: a politics of location and an overall search for that which is considered authentic. The language used to express these concerns is also quite compelling, when we consider the way in which language is at the heart of many of the controversies that have engulfed hip hop over time.

There are some astute style distinctions that demonstrate this. For instance, there is a long-standing and documented regional difference between East Coast and West Coast hip hop, which has been increasingly augmented lately by an equally distinct southern style. These differences are expressed through lyrics, themes, even something as personal as the accent one develops when rapping. One could break these regional differences down even further into local differences as well; the neighborhood one is from, the projects one grew up in, the differences between LA and Oakland, or New Orleans and Atlanta. It is precisely this series of moves from the local, to the regional, to the national, and even on to the global that demonstrates this expression of hip hop's cultural identity in the broadest sense, confounding any attempts to read Blackness as monolithic.

Ultimately, hip hop's concern with cultural identity has been about affirming authenticity, in what would otherwise be considered a postmodern, technologically driven, media-dominated, artificial world. To "keep it real" means to remain true to what is assumed to be the dictates of one's cultural identity. Although there are very strict rules in regard to what counts as being real, this quest for authenticity often translates to one's perception in the marketplace. It also has to do with one's relationship to capital.

Can hip hop serve two masters? Is it possible for hip hop to remain true to its roots, and at the same time still be popular? With hip hop now regularly displayed on MTV and other mainstream venues, it is unlike the early days when it was confined exclusively to the subculture. Now many within hip hop have expressed doubts about the public's newfound fascination with this once esoteric phenomenon.

At some level, what we are dealing with is an inherent dilemma of modern times. How does a nation so divided on the issues of race produce a definitely alternative form of culture to address the problems and despair that has consumed Black America in the post–civil rights era and this culture's slowly becoming part of mainstream America in the process? Using hip hop as a cipher *The New H.N.I.C.* will analyze this most compelling form of culture as artistic expression, political debate, social implication, and historical moment.

Peep the Scene

Using the comedy of Chris Rock as the opening salvo, the chapter "No Time for Fake Niggas" begins with an intricate analysis of the way that Rock, through language, and in the hip hop tradition of "keepin' it real," breaks down some of the oppressive tenets that have for too long restrained conversation around issues of Blackness when dominated by the civil rights generation. To the extent that the generation imposed a strict code of acceptable speech, Chris Rock and, by extension, hip hop itself attempt to undermine these limitations. His use of the so-called N word is but one example of how this plays out.

Rock's willingness to expose what were thought to be private conversations among Blacks, and his somewhat less than politically correct stance on these issues is progressive in that it allows for the discourse to be held in public and thus be more open than the private conversations that have tended to reproduce a cultural stalemate. His comedy is a strong example of how hip hop attempts to knock down the walls of complacency around what is considered acceptable Black discourse and how hip hop, through language, forces a reconsideration of the accepted privatized silence that often accompanied the civil rights imperative of acceptable behavior.

At some level though, the knocking down of these walls confirms the fact that hip hop is always already locked in a quest for authenticity, and this quest is often defined around the parameters of two distinct approaches toward achieving this desired sense of the authentic.

In the chapter "Brothas Gonna Work It Out," these two philosophies are revealed as they demonstrate the various strands that illuminate hip hop's identity politics and how this again differs from the civil rights model.

On one side are those who see a concerted political aesthetic to be the only fruitful path toward authentic existence in Black America. This side is often represented by a group of conscious rappers who bemoan the passing of time since the lost heyday of politically progressive hip hop in the late 1980s and early 1990s.

On the other side are those who see the pursuit of capital as the only true means to an authentic existence in America. These figures see the accumulation of wealth and material possessions to be significant in articulating their own sense of identity. Considering the odds of success for poor urban Black people in a hostile society, they see their triumph over these obstacles to be a political journey in and of itself, albeit a very different sense of what should be considered truly political is clearly being forwarded here.

This sense of the authentic has connections to several other factors but, most especially, it is about African American identity in the post–civil rights era. What does "to sell out" mean for African Americans growing up in the post–civil rights era and how has this influenced the culture that they have produced? Terms like "mainstream" and "crossover" have very distinct racial connotations about the audience in relationship to this question.

The idea of selling out can exist only in opposition to so- called real hip hop, which attempts to remain specific to the subculture, and has no interest in transcending it. These are the hip hop purists, and like the purist of any genre, they regard the celebration of wealth and material goods to be counter to hip hop's overall objective, which is to make music for the margins, as opposed to the mainstream. This is appropriate for this juncture in the music's history, for the need to reaffirm the overall mission of the culture is important precisely at this time of such mass acceptance.

Furthering this discussion around authentic identity, then, "Cant' Knock the Hustle" sees the pursuit of capital, the desire to "get money," as being central to any contemporary discussion of authenticity and it goes on to point out how the contempt for young Black men with money has come to be one of the biggest sources of friction in the hip hop era, both within hip hop culture and in the outside world as well. Recognizing that America has never had to reconcile what to do with young Black men and money in large numbers, this chapter attempts to unearth the reasons that this proposition is so troubling to so many.

Though hip hop is an overwhelmingly Black male space, "Head Nigga in Charge" will look at the way that hip hop and its cross- cultural influence have also come to alter popular representation of the White male as well. Of particular interest, is the fact that White teenage suburban males are said to be the largest purchasing market segment in hip hop culture. To what extent does this audience segment inform hip hop culture?

Norman Mailer's 1957 article, "The White Negro," opened discussion of an alternative White masculinity, uniquely informed by the Black culture of the day, particularly jazz. Former president Bill Clinton is a magnet for the way in which questions of racial identity and appropriation have emerged in contemporary discussions of White culture and its debt to the Black aesthetic. It is not surprising, then, that these questions have also consistently emerged during the time of Clinton's presidency.

Contemporary culture has also seen a recent rebirth of this character across popular culture in film, television, music, and basketball, among other places in society. Cinematic examples would include figures like Jack Nicholson, John Travolta, Warren Beatty, Johnny Depp, Bruce Willis, and George Clooney. And the recent popularity of musical figures like Eminem, Bubba Sparkxxx, Kid Rock, Korn, Limp Biskit, and basketball player Jason Williams—nicknamed "White Chocolate"—demonstrates the prevalence of this trend among a younger generation.

Do all of these White figures simply colonize Blackness, as was the case in the past, for their use or is this a testament to the contemporary power of the Black male image, and a reversal of previous racial politics? Central to this chapter, then, are questions of appropriation and power. Warren Beatty's racial politics, as represented in the film *Bulworth* (1998), for instance, force us to ask to what extent do the continued attempts by White figures to appropriate Black culture reaffirm dominant racial hierarchies? Or to what extent do these attempts offer contemporary examples of a realignment of power brought on by the normalizing of race in hip hop, and this influence throughout the culture?

In essence, hip hop and basketball are spaces where Blackness has been normalized, and Whiteness treated as The Other. Of course, this is completely opposite to the way in which race tends to function in more mainstream spaces. By investigating these spaces, we can begin to look at the power relations specific to sectors of this landscape, and expand the discourse around the culture in the process.

During the early part of 1999, Detroit rapper Eminem emerged as another prominent example of a longer historical trend in music, that of White performers attempting to be accepted as "legitimate" in a normally Black idiom. Unlike previous White rappers, though, Eminem's (Slim Shady) debut record *My Name Is* not only appeared high on the pop charts but was also taken seriously by the core hip hop audience as an album by a White artist. This is unlike, say, Vanilla Ice, whose short-lived popularity in the early '90s, was roundly scoffed at as a crass attempt toward exploitation. Slim Shady was being discussed for his rap skills, as opposed to simply being a situation emblematic of an underlying racial discussion. Shady's close association with rap impresario Dr. Dre, as his producer, certainly assisted in developing the perception that his music is "legitimate."

To what extent does the presence of White rappers augment the racial politics assumed to be specific to hip hop? Was this situation inevitable, considering that suburban White male teenagers constitute a larger segment of the rap audience and that the music is so prominently displayed on numerous mainstream cultural outlets? How is this sense of appropriation different from what it might have been in a previous historical era?

So, with this in mind, relax yourself, let your conscious be free, get wit the mind of Dr. B.

1 No Time for Fake Niggas

Hip Hop, from Private to Public

I came to bring the pain/hardcore to the brain.

—Method Man, "Bring the Pain"

Choppin' Up Game

As long as I can remember, my father and several of his friends would get together on Saturday morning for a lively breakfast. Over the years the restaurant locations have changed constantly, and the participants have tended to come and go, depending on what was happening in people's personal lives at a given time. What was constant was the intense conversations that would take place around the breakfast table. I have been fortunate on many occasions to be able to witness these breakfast sessions as an interested observer.

The meetings were certainly generationally specific, thus my words were limited to a few because I was simply too young to get in this game. It was not my place, and I never had a problem being quiet and listening, taking everything in like Absorbine Jr. These conversations were fascinating to me, so much so that I have tried to re-create the same atmosphere with several of my own friends over the years.

Their breakfasts would usually begin with my father's playing Cannonball Adderly's classic "Mercy, Mercy, Mercy" on the jukebox. This was like the sounding of the bell, so to speak. Let the games begin! The topics could range from the purchase of someone's new car to some recent sporting event, but most often the conversations would have to do with race and race relations in America. These men, most of whom were born before 1940, had a very distinct view of the world, and though they seldom came to a consensus, the discourse itself was fascinating. Some of these men were Black Nationalists, some of them were Republicans, most of them were somewhere in between those two poles. This is what made for the lively give-and-take.

What was so important about these discussions was that they had a certain sense of freedom to them. The men were free to express their beliefs openly. You might get clowned for saying some bullshit, you might get dismissed as an Uncle Tom, regardless, it was open, and everyone knew the unwritten rules. Say what you want, just be able to defend what you say.

The freedom of the exchange had to do with the fact that these were discussions, in essence being held in private, although in public places. It was the men's conversation, and no one else was listening. They could say what they wanted and, of course, this was not the case as it pertained to their place in mainstream America; certainly it was not the case when one considers the time they came up as Black men. Here they were free to discuss whatever, without the eye or ear of the proverbial "White man" interfering in any way. This is what made the conversations so lively; the freedom to say what the fuck you wanted to say, without fear of any sort of retribution or consequences for your words.

I am happy to tell you that most of what they had to say, sounded very much like Chris Rock.

In a society where the Black voice is often muted if not downright silent, these Saturday morning breakfast discussions were just the opposite. They were loud, boisterous, and quite insightful as well. It was as though these men were providing the commentary that had often been missing from the one-sided presentation that Black people received in the mainstream media. Although the conversations were decidedly pro Black, it was not beyond these men to criticize their own people. As a matter of fact, this was a featured point of the discussions.

Their criticisms, however, were spoken in the spirit of love, however biting they may have been. It was as though the mainstream was not getting it right because its agenda was suspect. The mainstream wanted to see Black people in a certain way. These men wanted to see Black people in a certain way too, but they used the negative always as a way of getting to the potential of the positive. It was understood that they came in love, not in anger or alienation, and it was expected that their comments be treated as such.

The furthest concerns from their minds were the thoughts of White people. They could not have cared less or, more to the point, they didn't give a fuck about a White person's opinion in these quarters. Considering the ever-watchful eye of the "White man" again, this was a rarified space, an exclusive space where the articulations of a distinctly Black discourse was the beginning, middle, and end of the discussion. This was an inherently private discussion and was intended to remain that way—thus the freedom of expression. As a matter of fact, my father was the only one liberal enough to even allow my young ears to hear what was being said. The others felt that this was simply too much for their young sons to hear. This was one of the only places where they could do their thing and they were not going to let anyone stop their flow.

Like these discussions among my father and his friends, much of what Black people say has been said in private. It is readily accepted for Black people of a certain generation that one had to put on a different face when dealing in White society, for one's real face was deemed unacceptable. This is because Black people must fit whatever limited range of images the mainstream has defined for them. There is no real regard or interest in learning what these people are really about; instead, it is about fulfilling a stereotype of one sort or another. Thus, as a way of survival, many Black people began donning an alternative persona, one devised for the purpose of existing in a hostile White world. This is especially true in a generational sense, where those who have the knowledge of a longer history know of the beatings, lynchings, and other brutalities often visited upon those people who refused to participate in this elaborate game of racial charade.

Accordingly, in order to express one's true feelings, these discussions often had to be held in private, where one would not have to look over his or her shoulder, or worry whether one's comments might cause the loss of one's job or, worst, one's life. This Black private space became a highly charged arena, then, a place where all those things that had been operating latently could be expressed openly, albeit away from the gaze and range of White society. In my mind, this is where the notion of the underground was formed, literally from the Underground Railroad, and figuratively as it moved throughout the rest of the culture.

Hip hop has come to be the contemporary cultural expression that most obviously has no problem being loud and clear. This is true of the music and it is also true of the way that many African Americans now see themselves. Though generationally there are still those who were raised under the old regime and who still maintain their undercover posture, many contemporary African Americans refuse to couch their language, style, or overall attitude. To do so now is to be something other than yourself, to be what is thought of as "fake," and of course, hip hop is all about "keepin' it real." What was often in the past said in private is now being regularly said in the most public of venues and hip hop has become the forum.

Why Blow up the Spot?

> I'm expressin' with my full capabilities/now I'm livin' in correctional facilities.
>
> —Dr. Dre (N.W.A.), "Express Yourself"

As N.W.A. said back in 1988, "Express Yourself"; in other words, freedom of speech is endemic to hip hop. Though it is important to be able to speak freely, many of this older generation have raised an objection to the openness of the hip hop's voice. Do you want people on the outside to hear *everything* you have to say? It gets back to an age-old Black question about whether it's appropriate to "put your business in the street."

It has long been thought that to criticize other Black people in public was to assist in one's own destruction. The argument goes that if you tear one another down in public, you are thought to be aiding and abetting the criminal enterprise of racism. It is felt that White society could use this against you and, moreover, it is simply thought to be in bad taste.

My father and his group engaged in their critique amongst themselves. No harm, no foul. No one else heard them anyway. Chris Rock, on the other hand, was right there on HBO and later on videotapes and DVDs for the world to hear. Though some of the same things were said, they were being said in public and this issue of public versus private was forced onto the agenda in a way that far transcended anything that had happened like this before.

Certainly, Richard Pryor spoke what had been unspeakable before he came on the scene. Yet, Pryor was talking about White people and their racism. Considering Pryor's own immersion in the politics of Black Power, his private tutorial under the direction of Huey Newton, and the politics swirling around those times, his contribution to the discourse was taking place within a broader context in which many African Americans were now getting a chance to openly engage in a critique of American racism for the first time.

Chris Rock, on the other hand, was talking about Black people and their pathologies to an audience that far superseded the primarily Black audience in attendance at the Tacoma Theater in Washington, D.C., that night in 1996. Some might suggest that many White people with less than noble intent might use the same criticisms that Rock made that evening against Black people. In this regard, Rock would be thought to cosign the racist stereotypes of poor Black people already held as true by a White establishment. The fact that another Black person was saying what many Whites felt but could not openly say gave credence to the view of African Americans as societal threat.

Rock was not affirming dominant views of Black people for a fawning White audience, though one cannot deny that the public nature of his discourse was available for all who would choose to use it in whatever fashion they desired. No, instead Rock was, in the spirit of old school cappin' and new school dissin' calling out his own people, signifyin' on them for some of their own self-inflicted wounds. He, like the gathering of older men mentioned already, came in love, and he spoke to his in-house audience that night as though they were all part of a larger public Black conversation. Similar to a president's State of the Union message but in a distinctly Black cultural style, complete with call and response, Chris Rock raps in an affirmative first- person plural to his well-schooled audience of brothas and sistas.

The show begins with Rock directly addressing this audience; he shouts out, "D.C.!!! Chocolate Ci-tay!!!" The setting for Rock's show is quite significant here in that Washington, D.C., is of course the nation's capital but more important because of its overwhelming Black population, it has also been called "Chocolate City." This appellation was originally used by funk master George Clinton back in the 1970s, when he pointed to the increasing White flight from major urban areas across the country as the birth of the "Chocolate City with its vanilla suburbs." "D.C.," as it has long been referred to by many African Americans, was thought to be the model Chocolate City. Because location is of utmost importance in hip hop, Rock makes this immediate connection. Then the fun begins.

Rock mentions D.C. as the home of the Million Man March, the massive political demonstration organized by Nation of Islam leader Louis Farrakhan in 1995. He says that all the positive Black leaders were there and goes on until he gets to D.C. mayor Marion Berry. In his signature exaggerated cadence Rock says, "Marion Berry, at the Million Man March. You know what that means? It means that even in our finest hour, we had a crack head on the stage."

Right off the bat Rock jumps into the mix, openly criticizing Berry who was convicted and jailed for smoking crack on camera, as part of an F.B.I. sting operation in the early 1990s. Rock inquires, "How the hell did Marion Berry get his job back?"

The political situation is indeed a delicate one. Berry was caught smoking crack on camera, true, but this came after a long and expensive federal entrapment mission into the mayor's personal life. Smoking crack is certainly not the image of a mayor any of us want to see. Berry was an open target for criticism, not the least of which was his colossal case of bad judgment. Yet, the effort put into this by the feds far outweighed the severity of what is at the end of the day a personal indiscretion. It is said that more than $40 million over a ten-year period was spent to finally show grainy video footage of the mayor begging the female informant for sex, while he himself was "sucking on that glass dick." It is hard to forget Berry's surprise when he realized it was a sting. He began yelling quite simply, "Goddamn, the bitch set me up!"

Rock is well aware of this history and chooses to go in a different direction with it. There is some distance between the original incident and the moment at which Rock speaks. His critique is rooted in the fact that Berry got reelected after serving jail time, that the people of D.C. demonstrated such bad judgment when reelecting a former crack user after the fact.

As a matter of fact, Berry was lampooned on *In Livin' Color* back in the early 1990s, not long after the initial event had taken place. This skit, with Keenan Ivory Wayans imitating talk show host Arsenio Hall and David Alan Grier playing Berry, was seen in one of the early episodes of the show. In one memorable passage, Wayans says to Grier, "I heard you got a new book and I hear it's smokin'!!!" to which Grier sheepishly responds, "No Arsenio, I was caught smokin' and I got booked." Again, there is a sort of insiders' humor to this skit that is certainly irreverent but is also quite funny considering the source. I suggest that a *Saturday Night Live* skit would not have been received the same way, because of all the racial connotations. The source and context of the critique make all the difference in the world.

Chris Rock, on Some Other Shit

Though many White listeners would be surprised at the honesty of Chris Rock's words, Black people have these sorts of discussions amongst themselves all the time. Again, it was the fact that many White people were listening, thus it was possible that these comments could now be used against Black people by those who were a lot less benevolent than Chris Rock was that evening.

For this reason, many African Americans have felt that Rock's words were out of place, that he was affirming dominant stereotypes of Black people, that his comments should not have been made with so many White people listening. His critics can also point to the amazing success that Rock would come to enjoy in the aftermath of these statements, which for his critics, suggests that Rock was now embraced by the mainstream simply because he was willing to criticize Black people.

I am sure many of these critics would also point to the 1998 *Vanity Fair* cover on which Rock provocatively appeared dressed like a Black clown in a traveling circus. For those who would hold these views, who believe that Rock's success is now only about being a pawn in the White man's game, please look deeper. At the core of this cultural moment is an important lesson about the function of race in the post–civil rights era especially because it informs the way that we define Blackness in this moment.

The show begins with a shot of Rock's dressing room door. As the door opens, the camera slowly pans down to frame the comedian's feet. His black-and-white "Spectator" shoes stand out. With this focus on the feet, Rock begins his stroll to the stage. A series of images begin to appear, superimposed over the strollin' "Spectators." The images are of classic comedy-album covers featuring a range of comedic talents, styles, and eras, and offering a broad historical backdrop against which to understand Rock's work. The album covers suggest a kind of comedy hall of fame and they also suggest a lineage and foreground the vast lexicon of comedy that has influenced a serious comic like Chris Rock. The album covers, in order, highlight some of America's most regarded comics: Bill Cosby, Dick Gregory, Flip Wilson (as Geraldine), Richard Pryor, Steve Martin, Pigmeat Markham, Woody Allen, and Eddie Murphy.

Rock connects himself to a lineage, a tradition, and his most interesting choices are figures like Pigmeat Markham, Steve Martin, and Woody Allen. In demonstrating a connection to an older though often controversial Black chitlin'-circuit comic tradition with Pigmeat, Rock also makes a connection to figures like Steve Martin and Woody Allen, who seem to exist outside the worldview of many of the other Black comics working today.

Rock's work is in contrast to what became of the originally spectacular *Def Comedy Jam* series on HBO. Though *Def Comedy* started out as a much-needed venue for the expression of Black comedy that was being ignored by the mainstream at the time, the show eventually ran its course and fell victim to an inferior group of comedians who tended to regard the idea of originality with contempt. These comedians began primarily recycling a series of worn-out clichés about Black sexual prowess, homosexuality, and supposed Black and White stylistic differences.

The redundancy of the routines coupled with the completely over-the-top audience participation soon made *Def Comedy* a caricature of what it had originally started out to be. So much so that, again, *In Livin' Color* did a famous skit on the show that featured, among other things, audience members laughing so hard that someone's head blew off in the process.

Whereas Rock's comedy was rooted in thought, the comedians on *Def Comedy* clearly got props for how outrageous they could be and how loud they could make the audience laugh. The difference is that Rock's work was about humor and wit, jokes that were not only funny but ultimately thought-provoking attempts to analyze a serious issue through the use of comedy. When hearing Rock and recognizing the potential truth, for instance, about the way that "ignorant ass niggas fuck things up," one has the tendency to laugh so as to keep from crying.

Def Comedy Jam, on the other hand, was not about humor, but was all about getting laughs—and there is a profound difference. Whatever outrageous things someone could say to get the audience to explode was considered par for the course. There was very little thought involved and the emphasis was more on the physical, thus playing to a very different audience and playing for a completely different set of laughs.

One could say similar things about BET's *Comic View,* which pursued as outrageous a course as did *Def Comedy* but could offer only a low-rent version of this, due to the fact that the comedians were restricted from using curse words because BET does not enjoy the same openness in this regard as HBO does. Thus these comedians tended to become even more physical and therefore much more stereotypical in their attempts to get laughs. As Rock himself stated in an article in *Billboard* magazine (September 28, 1996), "A lot of them don't study jokes, but do real bad versions of Richard and Eddie."

To compound matters, the show, which was always taped in Los Angeles, moved to Atlanta in the late 1990s in order to avoid the wrath of the labor unions in LA. BET paid a minimal wage to the comedians and refused to pay residuals for repeat broadcasts of the programs. Often the show would simply be an edited collection of previous performances anyway, so the offense here is even greater when one considers that it was getting by cheaply on the reruns, and then it was revealed that they were not even paying residuals.

Chris Rock's work is also of a perspective different from that of, say, film comedians like Chris Tucker or Martin Lawrence, who, in their tribute to Stepin Fetchit reaffirm some of the oldest stereotypes about Black performance that one could imagine. Rock is also quite different from the comedians represented in *The Original Kings of Comedy* (2000). These comedians, Steve Harvey, Cedric the Entertainer, Bernie Mac, and D. L. Hughly, all of whom are indebted to the late underground comic genius Robin Harris, became visible on either *Def Comedy Jam* or *Comic View* and then branched off to their own separate projects. Yet they also would come together to form a comedy force theretofore unrivaled. The so-called Kings of Comedy tour was an immense success, playing for multiple nights and to sold out arenas throughout the country, yet the tour was known only to Black audiences. The film of the tour went on to post incredible box office numbers and reach a crossover audience.

Here the comedians are much more conservative than their *Def Comedy Jam* counterparts, though an all-Black audience is implicit in their address. Yet their address is distinguished by the generational and class differences inherent to this audience. Whereas *Def Comedy* assumed a hip hop posture in its generationally specific address to its audience, the Kings of Comedy was very much a working- or middle-class address, rooted in an old school R&B sensibility, often either critiquing hip hop or overtly distancing themselves from hip hop in the process.

Chris Rock, on the other hand, combined elements of all these modes of address but by "tricking off" his performance with the inclusion of a broader range of influences, distanced himself from the crowd and ultimately transcended the imposed limits of such a specific audience.

Is It Somethin' I Said?

Although many may have felt that Rock's comedy was inappropriate for non-Black audiences, there is another reading that must be extended here. For too long Blacks have been thought of as a singular group of people who are often perceived to think and act the same on all issues. This lumping together of all things Black in the minds of many Americans, is at the root of racial representation in this society. Whereas, Whiteness often assumes a certain individuality in its representation, the act of one Black person is often regarded as representative of an entire group of people, particularly if that act is negative. Not only is this the case as it pertains to dominant White perception, it is also true in the case of many African Americans. There is an unspoken definition of what can be encompassed under the heading "Black," and anyone who does not fit in accordingly is often dismissed for failure to live up to the standards. Am I Black Enough For You? Indeed!

What Rock does with his critiques is expose the fact that, in essence, not all Black people are alike. By expressing his contempt for "niggas," and juxtaposing this against his love for "Black people," he is clearly suggesting that this singular approach will no longer hold up under the weight of contemporary society. It is important to recognize the differences that divide Black people, while understanding the historical circumstances that would make for a united front in the first place.

There was a time in America when all Black people, regardless of class status, had to occupy the same physical space. This, of course, had to do with the legally justified segregation that pervaded the land in one form or another. At this time, the idea of community was quite accurate, in that there was a stratified representation of the people who inhabited the space. Yet, the point at which people with the proper resources could move to other places, and the only people remaining were those who could not afford to move, is the point at which this community ceased to exist, at least in a physical, racially exclusive sense.

When you consider the prevalence of Black culture throughout America, it is possible to imagine a community based on cultural representation, but one cannot suggest that there remains this traditional sense of community now that class status defines who occupies the space in question. In other words, there is no longer a Black community, or at least not one solely defined by race.

Identity in this society is much too complicated now to assume that there is only one element at work in the definition. It is important to recognize the influence of race, alongside issues of gender, class, sexuality, generation, and even location, as the geographically specific nature of hip hop has demonstrated to us repeatedly. Though there remain those who choose to see the world only in shades of Black and White, I would suggest that this is a very limited perspective from which to observe. As population shifts redefine how we understand the question of race in America, it is important that our sense of identity and our cultural criticism follow along with these changes.

While the Black/White racial distinction is at the core of America's existence, and for this reason will always have a strong influence on the culture as a whole, this is no longer the sole reality and therefore cannot be used to answer all questions. The different realities of, say, Asian Americans or Latinos cannot be simply condensed or dismissed in order to accommodate the dominant order. Their realities must be accepted as such, and allowed to exist without being subsumed under some traditional category just for the sake of convenience.

In making the distinctions that he does, Chris Rock points out a very important fact, and in doing so, he suggests that all Black people cannot be assumed to exist along the same axis. To have said so in the public way that he does implies to all watching that Black people are not all the same and thus opens the way for a broader understanding.

There have always been those who would say for instance that we should not separate Martin Luther King Jr. and Malcolm X because their aims were similar, though their methods might have been different. Yet, it is important to separate them because they were different in ideology and approach and it is important for people to understand that these differences exist in the Black community. This recognition forces people to see a broader picture, as opposed to seeing things in such a monolithic way. This recognizes Black people as complicated, instead of the simplicity that many pursue in order to understand this representation.

There is a certain honesty to Rock's words that are definitely influenced by the openness that hip hop has fostered in the culture at large. In that hip hop is about the expression of one's individuality, its reliance on a discourse of the real embraces a certain articulation of things deemed "truthful." Rock is "keepin' it real" by choosing not to hide behind the veil of what is socially or racially acceptable. He is saying what needs to be said about issues of race, in spite of the fact that in this contemporary climate of political correctness, issues of this nature are often couched in a discourse that regards any mention of race to be rude and inappropriate or, worse, the issues go without being discussed at all. It is important to point out that even though the issues go ignored, they can in no way be said to truly disappear.

Though Rock's words are certainly there to be appropriated by the mainstream and can be used to justify all sorts of racial perceptions, this is in no way a reason not to have said what was spoken. One must recognize that in a media climate like that of today, culture is there for the taking, and because so many people have access, the possibilities for appropriation are infinite. This is the reality and is to be accepted.

There is nothing we can do to stop young suburban White teenagers from wanting to imitate the posture of a gangsta rapper. In the same way, there is nothing we can do about some ill-intentioned White person's using the words of Rock to justify his or her own racism. Rock did not create the racism; he simply exposed some of its impact. Therefore, his articulation of these pathologies is significant and can be said to knock down the wall of silence that for too long had limited the opportunity to understand these issues in a more sophisticated way.

Strictly 4 My Niggas

Rock's openness in regard to critiquing his own people is not unlike the controversy that continues to swirl around the use of the so-called N word. Certainly since the O. J. Simpson trial in the mid 1990s, America has been divided over the controversy surrounding the word "nigger" and its more recent transformation into "nigga." One can date the invention of this locution, the "N word," directly back to this historical moment. Yet, hip hop culture has certainly used the word extensively, and this is what has prompted the ongoing debates.

There are many who feel that the word should not be used at all, and others who feel that the word should be used only by African Americans. Many Black gatekeepers feel that the word is an awful reminder of the past and want it to be censored, and many Whites feel that it is unfair to have a word that African Americans can use and White people cannot. Hip hop though, rejects both postures.

"Nigga" has become a reworking of the original concept. The hip hop generation has reclaimed this word and in using it, they forward its multiple possibilities. It can, of course, be a term of endearment, such as it is used by someone like DMX in his famous cut, "My Niggas."

> Just cause I/love my niggas/I shed blood/for my niggas/let a nigga holla/where my niggas?/All I wanna hear/is right here my niggas!

In this regard, his use of the word is akin to "brothers" or "friends"; it connotes an undying solidarity, a loyalty unsurpassed by anything else.

DMX also performed this song during the 1999 Woodstock festival to roaring applause. The audience at the Woodstock event was overwhelmingly White, of course, and DMX was one of the only Black artists to perform at the event. The cut "My Niggas" features a call-and-response style, in which the crowd chants the words "My niggas," while X himself, fills in the various response "some niggas that you don't wanna try/who'll have you cowards ready to cry. . . ." Of course, the sight of five hundred thousand–plus drunken and doped up White kids yelling "my niggas" at the top of their lungs is not the sort of image that conjures up warm fuzzy feelings of love. There is something incredibly frightening about this as it evokes historical imagery of moblike violence in its racial ramifications.

This, too, is not unlike Oliver Stone's use of this same song in his extremely problematic film *Any Given Sunday* (1999), which affirms long-held stereotypes about the "natural" athletic nature of Black players, and their equally "natural" mental inferiority. Stone uses the song to imply that the mostly Black members of the Miami Sharks football team are coach Tony D'Amato's "niggas." The D'Amato character, played by Al Pacino, is in a struggle with Jamie Fox's character Willie Beaman ("Be a man") over control of his team. This charged racial dynamic, along with another challenge from female owner Cameron Diaz's character Christina Pagniachi, firmly endorses the idea of the White man victimized on all sides by either the threat of Black male physical dominance or White female financial control.

Thus, the use of "My Niggas" implies that the players are field hands and that D'Amato is the overseer. When the song is heard on the soundtrack, the film features a series of images, highlights, in which the Black players perform for their White coach and the adoring White fans.

In both cases, Woodstock and *Any Given Sunday*, DMX's words of endearment are used in ways other than to affirm a strong sense of Black unity. The connotations are quite different when used in conjunction with a White agenda. Yet, one cannot blame DMX for giving White people license to use these words. No, Whiteness is such that it needs no license, for it is the source of all power in America.

Whether or not DMX sang his song, the word would still have been in the lexicon of history, and available for usage. In addition, the racism implied in the usage of the word forms the backdrop against which race is understood in America. DMX did not create racism, nor can he access its power to discriminate. If anything, he is victimized by it. No, he can respond only to what he has been given and here his use of the word is a counter to its original meaning. He has used language as a way of asserting his own sense of identity, confirming that hip hop is, at its core, this battle over language and representation, which recognizes that words are not fixed but instead evolve over time to take on various meanings.

DMX realizes a certain freedom and liberatory potential in his use of language, and by embracing "nigga," he suggests that though ultimate power in America always lies in White hands that he can assert some semblance of power by his control of the words that come out of his mouth. His ability to define and re-define language is representative of the significance that hip hop now holds in relation to issues of power as they exist in contemporary American culture.

To live is to suffer. To survive is to find meaning in the suffering.

—DMX, Prologue to "Slippin"

In addition to this aspect, it seems that what underlies the controversy around use of the word in question is that this is a situation where White people are potentially prohibited from using a word that Black people now control. Some would suggest that this represents a double standard, but it is only one small example of the societal double standard that Black people have to accept if they are to live and survive in America. In no way does the denial of White people the right to use this word alter the balance of power in America and in no way does it diminish racism. It simply exposes a rare situation where the progress of Blackness holds a strong position relative to popular discourse. Ultimately, as both Woodstock and Oliver Stone suggest, no one can stop White people from using the word anyway.

What is important is that we get at the situation that makes this word so controversial in the first place, which, of course, is racism. To deny use of the word is to sweep it under the rug, to basically censor it solves nothing. It is not as though if we stopped saying the word today, that racism would disappear.

America already seems fixed on racism's being a thing of the past as a number of recent popular Hollywood movies like *Amistad* (1997), *The Green Mile* (1999), *The Legend of Bagger Vance* (1999), *Hurricane* (1999), and *Men of Honor* (2000), along with the revisionist reading of a film like *Ali* (2001), would suggest. It is often assumed in this media-dominated society that only the ubiquitous images of dogs and waterhoses can support claims of racial discrimination. Considering that these images, with some notable exceptions, are few and far between in the present, people assume that racism has disappeared. Yet, the discourse of racism remains quite strong and its subtle nuances are often invisible to those who refuse to get beyond this historical imagery as the only expression of such heinous treatment. It is this unsophisticated analysis of race and racism that informs these retrograde readings of the use of the word "nigga" and that continue to influence our understanding of how this issue is articulated in the present. Thus, repeated use of the word with impunity by many African Americans, through hip hop culture, exposes this complicated racial scenario for what it really is, the same old shit, simply a different toilet.

Race Card Monty

Ultimately there is a great purpose served by hip hop and, by extension, someone like Chris Rock who chooses to break down the barriers that often stifle our discussion of volatile issues like race and racism. Another common reference since the O. J. Simpson trial has been the use of the term "the race card." Often when African Americans choose to bring up race, they are chided by this now commonly accepted phrase.

Well, race is not a game, and it is certainly not something that you can play. This suggestion implies that the person who brings up race is really using it to "trump" others from arguing against this. The introduction of the race card into a discussion is considered not only inappropriate but also unfair. It is as though race has no place in the discussion and to bring it up, to merely mention it, is to break all the codes of socially acceptable decorum. In other words, it suggests that race has nothing to do with the issue at hand; unless someone arbitrarily applies it, as if it had not been mentioned, no one would have ever thought about it in the first place.

Of course, for those people who are defined by race, this issue is ever present and in no way arbitrary. One attempts to enter this in the discourse because its overwhelming absence is often the root of racism. The constant battle over representation is fraught with trying to have race be included in the larger conversation, where it has been ignored for far too long. Race is not a card you can use to stifle an otherwise neutral discussion; instead, it is a reality that defines the life of so many people who are in an ongoing struggle to be represented in their own way.

Hip hop has been quite instructive in this regard, and if we appropriate the language properly here, hip hop is a place where the race card is always being played. It is one of the few places in society where we can hear an ongoing discussion about race. Here, the walls have been torn down, the floodgates flung open. The once-private nature of Black existence has been replaced by a very public presence now. This reveals the good, the bad, and the ugly as to hip hop culture, and this openness can only be useful, for the lack of a discussion means a lack of attention and can be no good for people who are defined by their race.

Chris Rock's words are another example of the opening up of the discourse. Rock has made comedic appearances on hip hop records, including a memorable turn on Method Man's *Tical 2000: Judgment Day*, in addition to declaring in the blurb for his friend Nelson George's book *Hip Hop America* that he "loves hip hop more than I love my mother." Rock's hip hop stance, though, has generated a lot of negativity, and it has also encouraged comments about the appropriateness of his verbal gestures. On the other hand, Rock's openness, to me, implies a certain freedom of expression, a liberated sense even as it pertains to what can and cannot be said.

Rock, like the hip hop that inspires him and that serves as a cultural backdrop for his comedy, has consistently challenged mainstream perception, be it Black or White. Tyranny is no good, wherever it comes from. So, in this regard, the idea of keepin' it real is welcomed and should be well received.

As a whole, our image of racism is still too closely tied to the civil rights era. Though the horrific images that we have come to know of this time are without a doubt forever significant, we have allowed this to cloud our understanding of the way that racism now functions in a much more subtle and discursive manner, though in no way less destructive. We have allowed the images of Martin Luther King Jr, Alabama, Mississippi, and George Wallace to block out all other manifestations of racism in the present day. It is as though we have become slaves to civil rights, both Black and White. So much so that many African Americans now hold so tight those memories that they have squeezed all the life out of them, and many Whites assume that the end of this era means the end of racism. For many African Americans this masochistic indulgence in the brutality of the past has even become a badge of honor.

Again, this is why hip hop is so important: it forces us to move on by knocking down these obstacles from the past, by breaking all those rules, in order to get past this novocaine-like relationship that so many have to civil rights and recognize the more nuanced forms of racism that continue to dominate our society. To me, this transition from civil rights to hip hop is akin to a line from an old Bohannon cut, "Wide Receiver": the first time we knocked on the door, this time we gonna kick the muthafucka in!

2 Brothas Gonna Work It Out

Hip Hop's Ongoing Search for the Real

> We went from pickin' cotton/to chain gang line choppin'/to beboppin'/to
> hip hoppin'/Blues People got the blue chip stock option/Invisible Man/got
> the whole world watchin'/We're in your house/high/low/east/west/all over
> your map/I'm givin' big props for this thing called hip hop/where you can
> either get paid or get shot.
>
> —Mos Def, "Hip Hop"

Put That Rap Shit Second and Hip Hop First

What is the difference between rap and hip hop? I have been asked that question
far too many times by those not hip to the game. When I was growing up in the
late '70s and early '80s, rap was what the few of us who listened to the music called
it. At some point in the early 1990s, around the same time that MC Hammer was
beginning to embarrass all of those who had originally embraced his "James Brown
on crack" routine, people began calling anything with two turntables and a microphone "rap," and thus it was now necessary for the culture to make clear distinctions between the real and the imitation.

Hammer would go on to drop the "MC" from his moniker, and in doing so,
distance himself and all other pop wannabes from the true hardcore hip hop
heads. Because hip hop could see that Hammer's all-out stage show, genie pants,
and weak rhyme schemes were only a short-lived moment, the culture wanted
nothing to do with this trite cotton candy that the music industry was selling to

the ignorant masses. Rap came to be associated with the pop charts and hip hop was that which stayed true to the genre's original urban underclass roots. The "true heads" as they are called in hip hop circles now wanted nothing to do with this thing called "rap."

Rap soon came to be a verb of designation, defining the act that an artist would do when on stage or in the studio. Hip Hop 101; rap is the act of rapping, spittin' rhymes over beats produced by a DJ. An MC not only is a master of ceremony in the traditional sense but is very much a "microphone controller," charged with the fundamental task of moving the crowd.

The word "rap" also came to denote the more popular aspects of the genre by the mainstream, and this label was also used by the true heads to call out anyone who was thought to be abandoning the culture's roots As the age-old assumption goes, as one becomes more popular or mainstream, the less politically engaged and substantive the music would become. Hip hop changed the game on this, though.

There have been several pop rappers, of course, from Hammer to Will Smith and most recently someone like Nelly, but this is to be expected. Yet, unlike in the past, hip hop did not sell out or change itself to become popular, the mainstream changed so as to accommodate the music. In response to the charge of going pop, Jay-Z, one of hip hop's only MCs to have both popular appeal and retain his street credibility, says, "I didn't cross over/I bought the suburbs to the 'hood/made 'em relate to your struggle/I made 'em love you." In other words, the music remained hard-core, yet the public became fascinated with this sensibility and took it from there.

The old way of thinking says that in order to be popular, one has to sell out. What underlies this is a sentiment that assumes that mainstream White society is not interested in Black culture and that the music industry is interested only to the extent that it can exploit a particular image for profit.

It has also been long held as a belief that in order for a Black person to make it in White society he or she must compromise himself or herself and fit into an acceptable nonthreatening image that reaffirms the dominance of the mainstream, as opposed to exerting any distinct progressive Black identity. If we take this deeper, it reveals a racial conundrum where metaphors like "whitewash" become quite appropriate.

The question becomes, can one be commercial and continue to be relevant at the same time? Is it possible to integrate into mainstream society without being tainted in the process? The assumption has long been that in order to cross over, one has in essence to sell one's soul and compromise one's art so as to attract the largest number of followers.

We need look only at the numerous examples throughout history to demonstrate the validity of this point. Would Michael Jackson be known as "The King of Pop" had he not made physically ambiguous his racially distinct features and spoken lyrics such as "[I]t don't matter if you're black or white"? How would Louis Armstrong be regarded had he not been so visibly coonin' and jeffin', been so overtly stereotypical in his stage performance?

This is not to suggest that these figures were not significant artists and that their success and popularity were not due to immense skill, but it is to suggest that their respective crossover appeal was certainly enhanced by the fact that they easily fit into an allotted image reserved for Black performers, and by extension, Black people.

These consistently dominant images are similar to the ones that tend to influence most thinking in regard to hip hop culture as well. How could a genre of music go from being ignored to being blamed as the scourge of all evil, to being one of the most influential forms of pop culture on the globe?

One could argue that, like jazz, hip hop went from being reviled to being revered, but the difference is that jazz, now thought of as high culture, came to be thought of in this way by virtue of rock and roll's assuming the place of most common prominence in American life. Since it is assumed that jazz is primarily "historical" music, it is now safe to understand it as artistic, considering that history often adds credibility to culture. Yet even in its day, jazz never sold large quantities of music, nor did it ever affect more than a small segment of the population. In spite of its highbrow appeal, jazz not only confronted many racial limitations but also ran into several class limitations as well. In spite of all the influence jazz has had on the culture as a whole, at the end of the day, jazz was still an urban phenomenon, which grew to become an art form that was enjoyed all over the world.

Hip hop, on the other hand, may have started as an urban phenomenon, but it has moved far beyond that. Although it is hard to imagine that jazz had any real influence below the Mason Dixon line during, say, the 1950s and 1960s, for southern jazzmen would have had to move to New York to really be involved, southern hip hop has become a genre unto itself.

In the South, hip hop ranges from the cosmic pimped-out nationalism of a brilliantly original group like Outkast to the capitalist overdose of the Cash Money Millionaires, and on to other images that represent everything from the Black college marching band tradition in the music of Trick Daddy to the proliferation of Black southern strip clubs as referenced by artists ranging from Luke, back in the day, to Mystical and Ludacris now.

Jazz also did not have the benefit of the music video, a cultural form that is almost consistent in age with that of hip hop. If you were to hear jazz back in the day, you had to be in New York or one of the other urban centers where the music was played. You could certainly hear it on the radio and you could purchase albums, but you could not see it on television in the way that hip hop has become a television staple. This is obvious, for instance, when you consider that Viacom purchased BET, an otherwise worthless venture until you consider as well that it is a cable network that offers as its primary programming music videos, with hip hop videos being a large percentage of those being aired. Viacom, which already owned MTV and VH1, now owns all of the music video channels, with the purchase of BET allowing it to add Black music to its monopoly of this side of the industry.

With the proliferation of hip hop in the digital age, people now have ready access to the music, regardless of where they might live. Though people in New York might be listening to M.O.P., while people in the Bay Area are reciting the slang of E 40, and people down south are tuned into Eight Ball and MJG, they are all listening to hip hop. Individuals in LA can take pride in cats like Dub C and Suga Free, yet these artists may get no play at all in Detroit, where Jay Dee and Slum Village reign supreme. Nonetheless, they are all again dealing with hip hop.

The point is this: hip hop is such that it has crossed all sorts of boundaries yet remains specific to its immediate context. The history of hip hop will forever be rooted in the local, for this is the fundamental part of its identity, but its movement forward allows any and all to place their own spin on it and, at the same time, connect to its overall emphasis.

In this regard, rap is what you do; hip hop is what you are. Rap is the act; hip hop is the culture.

The culture of hip hop is composed of certain elements, these include MCin', DJin', break dancing, and graffiti art, among related others. These connections are best represented in the hip hop cinema classic *Wild Style* (1984). As hip hop has grown from its early South Bronx roots, though, it has come to be dominated by MCs and DJs. In my mind, these are the primary elements.

The Pimp Stick or the Pulpit?

Hip hop is concerned with self-expression in a world where the voice of young Black and Brown people are often mute. It is inherently about the "I," which is an attempt to distinguish oneself from the crowd, when identity is so often conflated to fit the demands of those in power. This is why "the 'hood" has become so prominent: it is the primary locale of one's existence. The idea of "representin'" has to do with self-expression and how this is also thought to be representative of one's place of origin. Representin' is active, and your place of origin central in defining your identity.

With this in mind, hip hop seems to have developed two distinct political views of the world, and these views have a history in African American culture. I have always found the root of these divergent political views to be most articulately expressed in a scene from the landmark film *The Mack* (1973).

The film's protagonist, Goldie, a ex con turned boss pimp, sits in a local park conferring with his brother, Olinga, a hard- nosed Black nationalist. The mellow sounds of Wille Hutch occupy the background and the tune is called aptly "Brothers Gonna Work it Out," a title later used by Public Enemy and a scene later parodied by Snoop.

The brothers are discussing their respective approaches to ghetto life and the possibilities of escaping such a doomed fate. Goldie sees the future through the lens of a Robin-in-the-'Hood- like entrepreneurial sensibility, arguing that his money and visible status are the keys to the future. His brother, on the other hand, suggests that Goldie's criminal exploits are part of the problem affecting Black people. Their conflict clearly represents the options thought to be the most viable to Black people in the aftermath of the civil rights and Black Power movements.

Olinga: You really don't understand do you? Hey man, in order for us to make this thing work, we gotta get rid of the pimps, pushers, and the prostitutes, and start all over again clean.

Goldie: Hey look nobody's pushin' me anywhere, ok. I mean, not you, not the cops, nobody man. You wanna get rid of the pushers, I'll help you, but don't send your people after me.

Olinga: Come on John, can't you see we can't get rid of one without gettin' rid of the other, we gotta come down on both of 'em at the same time in order for this thing to work for the people.

Goldie: Hey look, nobody's closin' me outta my business.

Olinga: Hey man, you my flesh and blood, you gonna make me make a decision I don't want to make John. You my brother man, can't you understand that?

Goldie: Being brothers ain't got nothin' to do with it man. I got a right to live my life the way I wanna live it. I mean, being rich and Black means something. Don't you know being poor and Black don't mean shit!

Goldie sees economic freedom to be the only solution and thus his criminal endeavors are perceived as the means to an end. He wants his brother to understand that his efforts are political, pointing out that when they were growing up there were no Black heroes and now he himself is considered a hero by some who want to emulate his lavish lifestyle. Goldie is simply saying that his money and the signs of his success, his cars, his clothes, even the prostitutes who "walk the track" for him are signs that he, a Black ex con, has made it in America when all other signs would have pointed to his continued demise. The fact that all the odds were against him, even makes it that much more of an important political statement.

His brother feels otherwise, that Goldie's life of crime is simply another expression of the way that the mainstream has forced Black people to live sordid lives. Goldie is a stereotype to him, doing exactly what he has been programmed to do by a unjust system. The fact that Goldie wallows in this makes his brother even more strident. He sees Goldie as a willing dupe in the White man's game, and this to him is indicative of the way that the Black community is being destroyed from the inside by its own pathologies and from the outside by the racism and White supremacy.

This debate has come to define much of contemporary Black life in America as well. What is the answer? Is it the at-times-tired rhetoric of civil rights and Black nationalism, or is it the ways of the criminal underworld? Which of these two will allow for those in the 'hood to move beyond their inferior circumstance?

We can see the update on this debate represented in Hype Williams's under-rated film *Belly* (1998) through the separate paths taken by the Nas and DMX char-acters. DMX, in one memorable soliloquy responds to Nas's encouragement to read about his history by declaring,

> Dog, come on wit the bullshit, man. You think another muthafucka know
> what you need to do? Ain't no purpose, Dog. It's money. We born to do
> fuckin' die, in the meantime, get money! Fuck a book!

Nas has pursued the life of enlightenment and has started to raise his conscious-ness. DMX, on the other hand, is concerned only with, as he states, "gettin' money" by any means necessary. The split between these two life options, *The Mack* and *Belly,* covers a long period of time and encompasses two of the most sig-nificant Black cultural representations during this historical period: blaxploitation and hip hop.

These distinctions between the political notions of Black nationalism and the underworld entrepreneurial ideas of "the life" can also be seen as the two most dominant voices in hip hop culture today. The struggles around the differences in these respective views now are as strident in the dialogue and discourse of hip hop as they have ever been.

There are generally two opposing camps when it comes to hip hop music. The gangsta camp, for instance, could be represented by figures like Jay-Z, Nas, Snoop, DMX, and Mobb Deep. These artists are often contrasted with a more overtly conscious political camp identified with artists like Common, Mos Def, The Roots, and Talib Kweli.

This is not to limit hip hop to these camps, for there are undoubtedly others that do not fit this equation. There is the comedy of someone like Redman, the af-firmation of the tradition by someone like Rahzell, or for lack of a better term, the alternative scene that features artists like Jurassic Five, Dialated Peoples, and the High and Mighty. Of course, I could go on to talk about the sexual provocation of

Lil' Kim or the womanist slant offered by Eve, but the primary debate and most visible forces within hip hop now tend to be either gangsta or political, and even these other variations are at some level connected to one or the other.

Although the gangsta camp is consumed with gettin' money, it tends to be less concerned with the political camp, though the political camp seems overtly concerned with the gangsta. In some ways the conscious rappers see the gangsta rappers as assuming all the attention and leaving the public to think that their underworld imagery is too pervasive. In the end, this is a class-specific argument that wants the negative imagery of lower-class gangsterism to disappear.

The history around this argument suggests that there was a time in the late '80s and early '90s when hip hop was overtly conscious and political. The group Public Enemy would serve as the model for this period. The argument goes on to say that with the advent of West Coast hip hop, and its emphasis on the gang bangin' lifestyle so endemic to southern California, that the music began to move away from this political period into a phase of unadulterated consumerism and a celebration of nihilism. It is further argued that the music industry was interested only in providing negative images of Black people, and thus a conspiracy to demean the race took precedence over the political aims of educating the masses.

This sentiment was first echoed by the Chicago rapper known at the time as Common Sense when he dropped "I Used to Love H.E.R." on his cult classic *Resurrection* in 1994. Eventually, he dropped the "Sense" from his name and going simply as Common raged against the machine of hip hop once again with his track "Doinit" from the *Like Water for Chocolate* album (2000). Here, Common suggests,

I don't give a fuck what you made in a year nigga/you wack/a soft nigga/on a hard track/in this new rap/generations of ex cats/like a Muslim/he fell off cause I pushed him/let his Bentley and his weak coupe be his cushion/I catch him on the street/in front of bodyguards and rush him.

As claims of yearly gross and records sold began to dominate the lyrics of many rappers, Common felt the need to strike back. His criticisms could be thought of as a veiled threat to figures like Puffy and Jay-Z; however, Common is defiantly referencing Will Smith.

Smith has in the past contracted both Puffy and Jay-Z to write lyrics for him. This practice of ghost writing hip hop lyrics is thought to be the worst thing one can do in a genre so tied into the originality of one's lyrics and style. Jay-Z outted this hidden practice some time ago, when he said, "S. Carter/ghost writer/and for the right price/I can even make yo' shit tighter!"

Common specifies his particular beef a bit more later in "Doinit" when he states, "[W]ith six degrees/I separate MC's/from a business man that's good/to a nigga that was raised/or just lived in the 'hood/from what a nigga say/to what's understood." The mention of "six degrees" is a direct reference to *Six Degrees of Separation* (1993), the film that launched Smith's Hollywood career. Common chooses to critique Will's immense bubblegum-like popularity, while at the same time he disses others who openly flaunt their newfound wealth.

Although something can certainly be said for the redundant nature that has at times consumed hip hop, especially as it pertains to the celebration of wealth, this lack of substance and originality can be expected. In any genre of music where the aim is to make money, there will inevitably be some music that is clearly weak and pitched to the lowest common denominator. This is why they call it "pop" music: its aims are to be popular at all costs. Will Smith is, for my money, definitely a pop artist of the highest and lowest order. Therefore Common's critique of Will Smith is on point, like Stacy Adams.

Smith's music represents the epitome of "rap" and is as far from hip hop as possible. Smith, who himself has gone on to critique hard-core hip hop in a now infamous Barbara Walters interview in 1998, is clearly using his larger-than-life movie stardom and his squeaky clean whitewashed image to help sell records. If anything, Smith has benefited from the controversy around hard-core hip hop because the media's negative image of this culture allows Smith to be the viable alternative. He has come out as critical of the hard-core artists who favor the "R"- and "X"-rated material, as opposed to his own "G"-rated bullshit. And here the "G" don't stand for gangsta either.

Here, I am even forced to invoke Eminem, who, in speaking to Will's lack of substance states, "Will Smith doesn't have to cuss to sell records/I do/so fuck Will Smith/and fuck you too." Thus Common makes a good point when singling out the imposter status of the man I like to call Lil' Willie, as opposed to the Big Willie moniker he tried to attach to himself at one point.

Will Smith, though, is a commercially successful pop figure who ultimately can be dismissed for his overall cultural insignificance. He has contributed nothing to the rap game; if anything, he has taken something from it. Smith is interested only in a connection to hip hop that might allow him to sell records, but he is not interested in being part of the culture.

Of course, Will Smith is not gangsta. The artists who fit under the gangsta banner, though, have become the targets of those who are politically minded. Talib Kweli states, for instance, "[T]hese niggas ain't thugs/the real thugs is the government/don't matter if you're Democrat/Independent/or Republican." The Roots have said it much more simply: "[Y]ou ain't sayin' nothin' new." In either case, the gangsta is being dissed as redundant.

I tend to look at this another way, though. The overwhelming popularity of gangsta rap has opened up the marketplace, and thus, these more conscious rappers have begun to get attention that was denied them before. Artists like Common, The Roots, and Mos Def can now get attention high on the pop charts that heretofore was not possible for acts thought to be underground. The popularity of gangsta rap has increased an awareness of hip hop as a whole, and this in turn has allowed for both sides to see profits. As opposed to seeing it as either/or, the success of genre has created the possibility for the success of hip hop itself.

Funny How Money Change a Situation

One need only witness the popularity and critical acclaim for Lauryn Hill at the 1999 Grammy Awards, where she collected five trophies that fateful evening. Hill's album *The Miseducation of Lauryn Hill* (1998) is neither pop nor insignificant; instead, it manages to merge the genres of hip hop with R&B and reggae to create a compelling combination that allows for her inspired, consciously womanist lyrics to stand out. Though the record was "popular" it was not "pop."

Hill silences any potential critics on her opening track, "Lost Ones," where she engages in one of the oldest hip hop traditions, the "battle rap." Here invoking the cutting sessions of an early jazz age, Hill "cuts" her former Fugees bandmate and reputed lover Wyclef Jean, declaring, "[I]t's funny how money change a situation/miscommunication leads to complication/my emancipation don't fit your equation." Here, Hill suggests that her association with Clef was such that she needed to be free, free to pursue her own agenda, in spite of his commercial aspirations. Hill sees Clef as being repressive of her voice. She declares in the hook of the song that "you might win some/but you just lost one."

Hill suggests that Clef's potentially exploitive use of her for financial and other gains has just ended. Any observer of The Fugees could see that it was Lauryn who had the real talent and recognize that this talent was being held back by Clef's demands. Thus Hill's departure from the group signaled not only a potential financial loss but a creative loss as well. Though Clef's records have done well, they are nothing when compared to Hill's phenomenal financial and innovative critical success.

Throughout the rest of the album, Hill is able to blend a succession of voices, a romantic voice, a spiritual voice, and a hip hop voice. Her lyrics on the track "Final Hour," for instance, clearly communicate her ability to flow in the truest hip hop sense. She also invokes a bit from the canon of flossin' that many conscious rappers would potentially shun.

In a particularly tight verse, Hill states, "Now I'ma get the mozzarella/like a Rockerfellar/still be in the church of Lalibela/singing hymns acappella/whether poised in Mirabella/in couture/or collectin' residuals from off The Score."

Her reference to "mozzarella" is quite interesting here. Mozzarella is, of course, cheese, and cheese is one of the most common ways that hip hop artists, especially gangsta artists, have referred to money. In other words, by invoking the gangstas' capitalist creed, she is definitely about gettin' money! She also suggests that her ability to get money is enhanced by her multiple skills, which include, modeling and also the collection of royalties off the first Fugee album, *The Score*.

Although this song is an overt nod to a spiritual quest—"you can get the money/you can get the power/but keep your eyes on/the final hour" she is saying that it is fine to pursue money but urges her listeners to do so with a purpose in mind. Hill can be somewhat self-righteous in her claims at times, but she recognizes the power of capital and points out that one must not get caught up in the chase and lose sight of the overall reason that capital is being pursued.

Hill's employment of a gangsta reference and her mad lyrical skills here suggest that she can move between several demands of the hip hop agenda. She is able to sing and flow with equal precision, and this is important because although there is a long history of Black female vocalists, from Bessie Smith to Jill Scott, one of the main criticisms of female rappers has been their inability to rhyme in the way that the male artists have defined as fundamental. Lauryn's lyrics and flow are unquestioned and, I think, are often overlooked because she is a woman, when the emphasis on her impeccable singing is what most people pay attention to. Her ability to reference the gangsta without necessarily dissing it is admirable in that the most creative artists have found a way to walk the line between the two, as opposed to embracing one while dismissing the other.

Welcome to Stankonia

The most successful in the attempt to fuse the two competing positions of gangsta and consciousness has been the group Outkast, who hail from Atlanta, better known as "The ATL." With the release in 1993 of their first album, *Southernplayal-isitcadillacfunkymusic,* Outkast introduced the world to their unique southern perspective. At this time, the only southern rapper of any note was the infamous Luke, the controversial leader of the 2 Live Crew, who had gained the spotlight as the target of one of the first "playa hatin'" episodes in hip hop history, when a south Florida prosecutor charged 2 Live Crew with obscenity.

Luke, though, was never—read never—a serious rap threat. His sex anthems "Me So Horny," "Throw That D," and "I Wanna Rock (Doo Doo Brown)" recognized the abundance of Black female bodies in the South and helped kick off the cult that now surrounds Black strip club culture as represented in a film like *The Players' Club* (1998). Luke certainly paved the way for the strip club genre of hip hop that has now had a strong expression from a number of rappers, again highlighted by the ever-popular Mystical and Ludacris. Yet Luke has never been known for his lyrical skills or his irresistible phat beats. In other words, Luke is wack, but he had a important momentary presence.

The other significant southern rap group in the early 1990s was the Houston-based Geto Boys, whose classic of hip hop paranoia "Mind Playin' Tricks on Me" still rocks every time you hear it. The Geto Boys were cool, especially Scarface, who is one of the better narrative technicians in hip hop history. Yet, even as Scarface stood out, the Geto Boys went through several incarnations and eventually faded as a group.

Outkast, though, offered an entirely different image. The group is composed of two members: Big Boi aka Daddy Fatstacks aka Lucious Leftfoot, and Dre aka Possum Alowishus Jenkins III aka Andre 3000.

What is important here is that the two represent both sides of the equation as it pertains to conscious hip hop and the gangsta aesthetic. Big Boi is a southern playa of the highest order; cool as if, in his words, he was "sippin' a milkshake in a snowstorm." Big Boi suggests in his stance that the idea of being cool and being from the South is not an oxymoron. His Savannah-drenched playa celebrations are famous in rap circles and his pimped out furs, gators, and vintage sports gear are a unique expression of southern style. Dre on the other hand, dresses in a wildly eclectic style that ranges from football shoulder pads and hula skirts to elaborate turbans. His lyrics are equally as otherworldly, showcasing a flair for the abstract though they remain clever and highly conscious.

Outkast made a strong showing in the fall of 1999 with the release of their third album, *Aquemini*, which suggested the fusion of Dre's and Big Boi's astrological signs, Aquarius and Gemini, but more important, suggested their bond together, their unbreakable merging of the two distinct hip hop styles. As articulated in the cut "Return of the Gangsta," Big Boi suggests that the two were "kinda like Mel Gibson and Danny Glover," underscoring the unique combination and the strength of its parts.

On the album's title track Dre drops an intellectual bomb from which the streets are still reeling. By posing a serious question, Dre asks,

Is every nigga with dreads for the cause?/Is every nigga wit gold for the fall/naw/so don't get caught up in appearances/it's Outkast/Aquemini/another Black experience.

Dre's point about image and appearance is well taken. Simply because someone wears dreadlocks, a style that of course references the consciousness and substance of Bob Marley and Rastafarian religion and the undeniably positive influence this has had in hip hop, does not mean that the person in question is committed to a progressive political agenda. Dreads, at the end of the day, like the Afro before them, are simply a style, a style now so prevalent that it is almost bereft of any real political substance.

On the other hand, the reference to gold here implies a gangsta-like aesthetic, one where diamonds or ice, and gators or alligator shoes are standard issue. Though platinum is the precious metal of choice in today's hip hop circles, the use of gold is still timely. From the days of Slick Rick's multiple, Mr. T–like collection of gold chains, to the present day of gold "fronts" that are often used as caps over people's teeth, excessive jewels have long been a staple of thug-life opulence. The wearer of gold, though, is no more an insignificant write-off than the wearer of dreads is a guaranteed conscious figure. Again, the gold is style, and nothing more. Though this style may connote several things due to appearance, it is ultimately one's actions that define these things.

Dre brings up a similar sentiment on Outkast's fourth album, *Stankonia* (2000), on a track entitled "Humble Mumble." Here he is speaking to a music critic who has been swept away by hip hop's negative publicity, though she knows very little about the music itself.

> I met a critic/I made her shit her draws/She said hip hop was only guns and alcohol/I said oh hell naw/but yet it's that too/you can't discriminate/cause you done read a book or two.

Here, Dre again is able to acknowledge the shortcomings of the culture, without dismissing it out of hand. He is saying that hip hop is indeed both gangsta and conscious, and that it is this combination that makes it so incredibly significant. Because no music or culture is without flaw, Dre responds to the double standard that many still continue to hold hip hop up to. Though there are many people who dismiss hip hop, most of them have never even listened to it. They go off on only what they have heard, and this ignorance of the culture, along with these shallow perceptions, tends to inform their jaded opinion.

Dre is arguing for a deeper understanding of the culture before one gets so caught up in dismissing it. Again, this is indicative of the way that Outkast have reconciled the two competing factions in hip hop and how their example can be a lesson to others still attempting to make it that dreaded either/or proposition.

Like most things in the culture, hip hop is neither Black nor White, and not simply good or bad. It does not fit into any neat and convenient category, for it is too complex for such a reductive reading. Instead, hip hop is dynamic. It is expressive of the ways of a generation, and in that, it moves across the spectrum, from high to low, from nice to evil, and everything in between. It is, without a doubt, the good, the bad, and the ugly of contemporary Black life in America, and in so being, it is the movement most equipped to handle the weight of Blackness in these times of such contention.

Hip hop often recognizes its own contradictions and in so doing is less about resolving those moments and more about embracing them. As opposed to the desire to make all of the culture fit into one neat, like, holding cell, groups like Outkast embrace the idea of difference and use difference as a strength instead of seeing it as a possible weakness. It is this dynamic, this sense of identity being multiple, that continues to make hip hop so relevant today.

Can't Knock the Hustle

Hip Hop and the Cult of Playa Hatin'

> My train of thought is that of a hustler/or a nigga wit his shirt off/tryin' to get his work off to customers.
>
> —Common, "Dooinit"

> Respect the game/that should be it/what you eat don't make me shit.
>
> —Jay-Z, "Heart of the City"

Fuck Y'all Analog Niggas, We Be Digital

One of the most compelling television moments in recent memory is the Clarence Thomas/Anita Hill Senate confirmation hearings of 1991. The precursor to what is commonly called "Reality TV," Thomas/Hill would whet our appetite for that ultimate blockbuster, the O.J. Simpson trial, which would come a few years later. The sweeping epic that developed around O.J., of course, would eclipse all other television dramas, both before and after, but it was the Thomas/Hill hearings that set the stage for the public by offering a real-life melodrama that, in many ways, exceeded the increasingly bland offerings available on network television at the time.

Just out of graduate school and needing to *come up*, I pursued my life as a professor in the only place that I could find willing to pay me at the time, the University of Utah. I spent a year of cultural house arrest in Salt Lake City, back in the early 1990s. I was living in SLC, and teaching my first course as a professor during the Thomas/Hill hearings.

I remember vividly one day, as the hearings became more entrenched, getting on an elevator in a downtown office building, when a White male Mormon proceeded to get on behind me. The gentleman, conveying his best permanently painted on smile, looks over at me and says, "How about our man Thomas? Hope he makes it. . . ." The gentleman got off the elevator before I could answer him, but I was left to ponder his statement disguised as a question. Our man Thomas?

To be honest, I originally thought that he was referring to Isiah Thomas (Zeke), the outstanding Detroit Piston point guard, who had recently been involved in an unfortunate encounter with Utah Jazz power forward Karl Malone's vicious elbow to the head that resulted in a some forty stitches over Zeke's eye. The blow came after Thomas had burned Jazz stalwart John Stockton for some forty-four points in a game earlier that season in Detroit. Since Zeke, one of the game's greatest point guards and floor leaders, had been curiously left off the original Dream Team and Stockton had been selected, many felt that the forty-four points was intended as a message to the world about who should have really been selected.

So upon the Pistons' visit to Utah that year, Karl Malone decided to send another message. Jumping to the defense of his White teammate, Malone, known as one of the "dirtiest" players in the league, next to Stockton that is, tried to blind Zeke with a lethal elbow to the head on one his drives to the basket. Blood poured from his head like a faucet that could not be turned off, and Zeke went to the hospital, only to return and finish the game.

Anyway, being from the "The D," I was a die-hard Piston fan who was still quite peeved that my man Zeke has been left off the Dream Team, and I was even more disturbed that Karl Malone had decided to jump to the defense of "the White man, " as it were. This was what was on my mind when the cat on the elevator asked me that question that day.

As I began to think to myself, "How does this guy know I'm from Detroit?" It dawned on me that he was not talking about Isiah Thomas at all. Instead, he was talking about the national obsession that had developed over these confirmation hearings. It was the gentleman's assumption that because Clarence Thomas was an African American, like me, that I, of course, would be a supporter. The gentleman embraced Thomas not because of Thomas's race but because his ultraconservative views were directly in line with the religious right's. Yet, he felt that these views combined with his race were enough to establish a bond between the two of us, for however brief that moment on the elevator might have been.

As the hearings developed, there was one point that would truly stand out for me. After an extensive day of questioning, an exasperated Thomas responded to his inquisitors that the confirmation process was really a "high tech lynching for uppity negroes." This quote would forever live on in the mind of the American public. It is no secret that many African Americans truly despise Clarence Thomas for his archconservative views. For many, Thomas is living embodiment of what was at one time called an "Uncle Tom," a Black person who was interested only in pleasing Whites and appealing to their sensibilities. Thomas, for others, was a sell-out, one who had benefited from affirmative action programs but who, now that he was on top, turned his back on his upbringing, his people, and his Blackness. These perceptions made the "high tech lynching" statement that much more controversial.

Many felt that because Thomas had abandoned his Blackness in pursuit of fame and power in the White world, he was no longer entitled to make claims of racism. It was as though he had given up his identity, and along with it, he had renounced all rights that come with it, including the right to point out racism when it appeared. How could he claim racism when so much of his professional life had been about denying the existence of this particular social evil? Many thought this to be hypocrisy of the highest order.

It is not my intention to defend Clarence Thomas, nor is it my intention to belittle the highly plausible claims of sexual harassment forwarded by Anita Hill. Black or White, Thomas is one of the most conservative Supreme Court justices ever to sit on the bench. Yet, this conservatism is somehow underscored by the fact that he is thought to represent a group of people, African Americans, who are often perceived to be overwhelmingly liberal and exclusively connected to the Democratic Party. Well, in actuality, Thomas's views are not that different from many other African Americans who have tended to be liberal in regard to issues surrounding race but who often are quite conservative on most other social issues, particularly when one factors in the dominant and consistently conservative influence of "the Black church."

I am, however, interested in the phrase used by Thomas to describe his predicament. First of all, he suggests that there is something "high tech" about this process that has him defending himself in front of several prominent senators, all of whom are White and male. This is the reification of "the White Man" in a most obvious way.

Here, Thomas also references the way that high technology would come to intercede in virtually every aspect of American life. In other words, there was something sophisticated about this version of racism, disguised by the overt professionalism of the process. The lynching in this case was discursive and rhetorical, as opposed to being physical.

He goes on to say that it is a "lynching for uppity negroes," invoking a reference from the past, with "uppity" being the word often used to justify all sorts of brutality against a Black person thought to be existing outside the box of his or her social class. In other words, the politically correct subtitles of the modern day were such that an overt physical lynching would be too obvious. Instead, one needed to develop a "high-tech" version, one not so easily visible to the naked cultural eye of America. In some ways, Thomas is suggesting that his accomplishments, his move beyond the normally confined spaces where Blackness might be allowed to exist, required something a bit more polished than simply a rope and a tree.

However insincere Thomas might have been in his use of this high-tech lynching metaphor, the function of the metaphor remains intact. It is a perfect way to describe the process by which mainstream American society often attempts to discipline and punish rich, visible, and powerful Black men in today's society. High-tech lynchings have become par for the course now that many African Americans have cracked the financial barriers that for so long were limited to White male exclusivity. As a matter of fact, Thomas was only the first in a long line of individuals who would be subjected to this type of public flogging, in spite of whether or not they were guilty or innocent of the charges.

In addition to O.J., these visible people would include, among others, hip hop figures like Snoop Dogg, Jay-Z, and Sean "Puff Daddy"/"P. Diddy" Coombs, along with football players Michael Irvin, Ray Lewis, and Rae Carruth, among others. Basketball player Chris Webber would also endure his share of this type of unwanted attention. In each case, a great deal of the discussion took place around their respective fortunes, their high-profile lifestyle, the legion of hangers-on they travel with, and ultimately their propensity toward violence. Far from simple court cases, and again, in spite of their respective guilt or innocence, these are all examples of the way that being Black and rich can be as much a detriment as a blessing. As Puffy himself has declared, it can be "mo' money, mo' problems."

This phenomenon has been best described by hip hop artist Mos Def on a track from his critically acclaimed 1999 album *Black on Both Sides*. The track, "Mr. Nigga," which uses an interpolation of an earlier A Tribe Called Quest song "Sucka Nigga," and features former Quest member Q-Tip, describes life at the top for those who happen to be young, Black, and rich: "[T]hey say they want you successful/but then they make it stressful/you start keepin' up the pace/they start changin' up the tempo."

Mos uses the name "Mr. Nigga" here, making a connection to a statement that Malcolm X would make on numerous occasions. Malcolm would rhetorically ask "What does the Klan call a Black man with a Ph.D.?" The answer would be "A nigger." Though Mos is able to modify the word with this contemporary spelling, he suggests that some things have not changed. In addition, Mos reminds us of an old Black adage that says mainstream White society often changes the rules in the middle of the game, so to speak, that whatever may be articulated as the "rules" of a given situation are always at the whim and discretion of those in power, and can be changed at any time to accommodate the views of the dominant order.

Mos goes on to say that what is considered "success" for Whites is often thought to be "suspect" when it comes to African Americans. Again, the suggestion of a double standard is paramount here. Underlying all of this is a belief that these wealthy Black celebrities have made it, that they have overcome many obstacles and their success for many Whites indicates that racism no longer exists. This is, of course, the same sentiment that was often expressed around the popularity of *The Cosby Show* in the 1980s, that the representation of this well-off Black family suggested that Blacks had become so accepted and concurrently so successful in the society that racism could no longer possibly exist. Their wealth was thought to be evidence to the contrary on the continued existence of a racist America.

In the game of capitalism, it seems to say that once you have become successful, then you are living proof that racism could not possibly exist; if it did, you would not have been so successful in the first place. The underside to this argument, though, is that capitalism is based on potentially benefiting individuals, but this in no way denies that those who are not White in this society tend to be judged by the perceptions of their group and not thought of as individuals at all. Therefore whatever money these celebrities happen to get tends to evaluated against the racist stereotypes, and people often question how they were able to achieve such money in the first place. This is the philosophy that tends to inform something like racial profiling, and it does not stop simply because one has made some money.

You Have the Playas and You Have the Playa Haters

There is nothing more potentially controversial in American society today than the idea of a Black man with money. Nothing.

There was time when the image of a Black man and White woman was considered the most volatile and threatening image to the dominant order. In many ways the racial hierarchy of the dirty South was predicated on denying the very possibility of this union. Not limited to the South, though, the march of history would offer numerous examples of how explosive this interracial situation really was, from boxer Jack Johnson's being indicted on the Mann Act to rumors of Sammy Davis's having his eye put out over dating actress Kim Novak, not to mention Vernon Jordan's being shot while jogging with a White female companion. Of course, much of the White anger expressed during the O. J. Simpson saga was rooted in this same fear.

In spite of these incidents, there are and continue to be enough interracial unions between Black men and White women that this issue, however problematic it may still be for some, is no longer exclusively the matter of life and death that it once was. If anything, society now often sees this union as a eroticized fantasy, often using images of this sort in advertising, for instance, and other areas of pop culture that seek to have an edge.

Yes, the threat once posed by the Black male/White female scenario has been replaced by the newly emergent image of the Black millionaire, and the hatred around these figures has escalated as the images have become more visible. From the basketball courts of the NBA to the recording studios of hip hop, and everywhere in between, Brothas with money have become easy targets for those who would prefer not to see them at all.

Those who have contempt for the highly visible Black millionaires are not only White, though, as the implications might suggest. No, these people, the "playa haters," if you will, are often other African Americans who express their open hostility toward the spectacle of Black money so often represented in the public arena. This sentiment can be heard, for instance, in the lyrics of Tupac's "How Do You Want It?" when, chiding one of hip hop's original playa haters, activist C. Delores Tucker, Pac declares, "Delores Tucker/you a muthafucka/'stead of tryin' to help a nigga/you destroy a Brotha/worst than the others." The point about being "worst than the others" refers to the way in which we often assume a certain racism from White society, but the internal hatred that circulates through Black discourse can have a devastating effect as well. It is in some ways like the old "crabs in a barrel" syndrome, amplified for the twenty-first century.

One of the results of racism has often been a self-hatred that has exaggerated internal tensions within Black circles, while distancing the concurrent rage from the real culprits, those forces in mainstream White society that work to keep Black people in an oppressed state. This self-hatred or as the hip hop cats have now termed it, "playa hatin'" continues to be a primary concern in the culture itself.

What I am suggesting here is not that we should be less concerned with racism, no. What I am suggesting is that the contemporary emergence of the playa hatin' phenomenon has complemented the already present racism with an unwitting, though capable ally. In other words, the contempt for Black men *gettin' money* as it were, is deep, complex, and multiple in the ways that it can potentially derail the continued possibilities of this economic progression.

On the same point, though, there is the example of the very public struggle between the National Basketball Association and the Players' Association during the lockout of 1998, which strongly suggests that it was a major concern that Black men were getting too much money and that something must be done to at least stagnate this process. When you consider that the NBA is a White corporation making money off Black labor, and that the public is well aware of players' salaries but has no idea what the owners make, the balance of power in this situation is pretty clear. Yet many refuse to see this situation in these terms because they feel uncomfortable embracing Black millionaires who are thought to be aloof, arrogant, greedy, ungrateful, and, in a word, uppity. Many people feel that Blacks should be grateful for even being in America and getting the opportunity to make so much money. This sentiment was echoed in 2001 when conservative charlatan David Horowitz ran an ad in several college newspapers suggesting that Blacks are not be entitled to reparations for slavery but instead owe a debt to America for freeing them from Africa, and giving them opportunity in America.

I also am reminded of a television campaign commercial for Los Angeles mayoral candidate Joel Wachs during the 2001 primary. The commercial features Wachs, who speaks in regard to the stance he took as a member of the city council on the issues of tax revenues for the Staples Center, the large new sports-and-entertainment facility in downtown Los Angeles. In an appeal to the so-called common citizen, Wachs states that the people's tax money should be not used to subsidize what he labels as "billionaire owners and gazillionaire players."

The most recognizable occupants of the Staples Center are, of course, the Los Angeles Lakers, one of the greatest basketball franchises in NBA history. With basketball being an overwhelmingly Black sport, any reference to the game recognizes this racial construction in its specific address. Considering this, Wachs's comments easily suggest that Black players are making more money than White owners.

This is obviously impossible and goes against every dictate of capitalism. Yet the suggestion can go unchallenged because it is commonly accepted that Black players are making far more than their deserved share. No business can afford to pay its employees more money than it takes in or bankruptcy will soon follow. This again goes against the very nature of capitalism. Yet with a situation like the NBA, it can be assumed that it is true that the players make more money than the owners because this sentiment plays to societal perceptions about overpaid Black athletes. The athletes are often discussed as though they were "stealing" the money, which, of course, reaffirms a dominant image of Black men and the perception of an inherently criminal culture.

This situation is a historically specific one, for the opportunity for numbers of young Black men to make money in ways visible to the public has come about only since the 1960s. This opportunity increased dramatically in the 1990s as hip hop became a driving force in mainstream society and in the music industry as well. Though we had been treated to the visibility of millionaire Black athletes for some time, hip hop offered another arena where cats who were thought to be uneducated and unskilled were able to move into a situation where they could make large sums of money and parade this before the television cameras. The difference here is that though Black athletes have often been made targets because of their wealth, the public appreciated, even desired, to see their continued presence on the playing fields.

In other words, America now loves its Black athletes; it simply does not want to pay them. Yet in the case of hip hop, many feel that the art form itself is suspect, so it is obvious that there remains contempt for the practitioners of this art form.

This contempt is enhanced when locating the situation within the ghetto, for these wealthy individuals are quite visible in contrast to the blight surrounding them. They become targets, both within their own environment and outside it. The dictates of the keepin' it real ethos demand that one continue to locate oneself in the 'hood, in spite of the material resources that would now allow one to leave. Biggie Smalls, for instance, proudly declared on *Ready to Die*, his first album, "[C]all the crib/same number/same 'hood/it's all good," but by the time of *Life After Death*, his second, he was saying, "[N]ow we buy homes in unfamiliar places," suggesting the difficulty that defined his life in the 'hood once he was visible and no longer strugglin'.

Or take for instance, the telling lyrics from Dr. Dre's opening track on his much-anticipated *Chronic 2001,* the follow-up to his seminal record, *The Chronic,* originally released in 1992. Considering Dre's very public history and his troubled relationship to the now-infamous Death Row Records head Suge Knight, many wondered aloud whether Dre would choose to speak of his storied past with the release of the new record, now that he had changed his image. The opening track on *Chronic 2001,* "The Watcher," which was, by the way, cowritten by Eminem, spells out how inconsistent Dre's new life was when compared with his old image. Here he poses the ultimate question in this regard: "I moved outta the 'hood/for good/you blame me?" He then goes on to say,

> How would you feel/if niggas wanted you killed?/you'd probably move to a new house/on a new hill/and choose a new spot/if niggas wanted you shot/I ain't a thug/how much Tupac in you, you got?/I ain't no bitch neither/it's either my life or your life/and I ain't leavin'/I like breathin'/so we can go round for round/clip for clip/go pound for pound/nigga if you really wanna take it there we can/just remember that you fuckin' wit a family man/I got a lot more to lose than you/remember that/when you wanna come and fill these shoes.

Here Dre explains how difficult, even life threatening, staying in the same environment can be as one attempts to rise to the top. At some point, moving forward is as much about safety and security as it is about wanting to indicate your newfound success by buying a large mansion. In this case, the idea of keepin' it real proves to be real, all right—as Chris Rock has said, "real ignorant." Those people who jealously critique someone like Biggie or Dre for moving out of such contested circumstances help to expose the image of the playa hater here in no uncertain terms.

The playa hater is an idea that has long been a part of the Black experience, but only during hip hop has it been given a name. The term "playa hater," or "playa hata," seems to have originated in Oakland and was put on record by a Bay Area group called The Luniz experiencing their fifteen minutes of fame during the summer of 1995 when their hot single and weed-smoking anthem "I Got Five on It" was dominating the charts and radio airplay. Their second single of that album, "Playa Hata," interpolated a hook from an early '90s Chuckii Booker single, "[W]hy you wanna, play your games on me?" changing it up by posing the question, "[W]hy you wanna playa hate on me?" Shortly thereafter, the term "playa hater" would become an instant classic.

If hip hop is about nothing else, it is about the redefinition of language. The way in which what was once called "Black English," and is now often referred to as "ebonics" has functioned in society has often been relegated to discussions of its usefulness, its appropriateness, and other questions about what is thought to be the incorrect use of the English language. Seldom has the discussion been about the way that these cultural improvisations on English alter the language in new and interesting ways.

Thus, in hip hop, verbs often function in a very active way. To "hate" on someone is to use the expressive powers of negativity to cast an aspersion on those who are visibly successful. To hate then becomes more than simply an attitude or silently held feeling of contempt. It is the active usage of that word. It is now common to hear people talk about someone hatin' on them. This, of course, is countered by the idea of "having love" for someone or something. Again, to "have love" would be thought to be incorrect English, by some; in hip hop, it is about an active and metaphoric sense of what would normally be thought of as love, for instance, "I got nothin' but love for you." With this active sense of love and hate in mind, one recognizes the way that playa hatin' has emerged as a primary concern in hip hop circles and has even moved beyond to suggest a larger systemic notion of this playa hatin' syndrome at work in mainstream society.

If The Luniz are credited with introducing the phrase to hip hop, then the explosion of the idea would center around the usage of this imagery in a legendary

Biggie Smalls track also entitled "Playa Hater." The track appears on the second disc of Biggie's classic *Life After Death* (1997). Using an interpolation of the soul standard "Hey Love," Biggie in a call-and-response hook with Keena Henson, a female background singer, croons his way, Nat King Cole–style, through the song. Near the end of the track, Biggie's erstwhile label head, Puffy, states, "Ya see, there are two kinds of people in the world today. You have the playas and you have the playa haters. Please don't hate me because I'm beautiful, baby." In the aftermath of Biggie's murder, it is Puffy with whom this sentiment would become most associated.

Puffy's dividing of the world into two equal halves, playas on one side, and playa haters on the other, would come to be a recurrent theme linked with his music-mogul image. His use of Kelly LeBrock's old Pantene shampoo commercial line, "[D]on't hate me because I'm beautiful," here shifts the focus from standard images of a subtle, though arrogant sense of female beauty to a not-so-subtle and still very arrogant notion of Puffy's wealth and material success. Yet, like Kelly Le-Brock, Puffy derides his critics by suggesting that their hatred of him lies in something he has no control over, his money. It is as though he is "naturally" wealthy in the same way that LeBrock was alluding to a natural sense of beauty, albeit enhanced by the powers of the shampoo.

Although mainstream society in reducing women to object status often enforces a standard image of female beauty, an enforcement that reaffirms a sexist hierarchy around women, especially those who do not fit the standard, LeBrock's commercial flips the script. She calls out, for instance, the feminists who would criticize this notion of a standard of beauty, by making them the perpetrators and making herself the victim. Seeing that those who are truly victimized rarely have access to the media, LeBrock controls the discourse, setting the agenda, making those who are innocent guilty, and making those who are guilty appear to be innocent. Puffy also seems to be blaming the victim, calling out those who would critique his success, and instead making them the aggressors, and making himself a victim of their jealousy. This martyrlike stance not only would add fuel to Puffy's critics but would have some very real-life implications as well.

In the spring of 1999 Puffy and several of his associates went to the office of Steve Stoute, a respected music industry figure and the manager of hip hop artist Nas. Puffy and his associates allegedly beat Stoute with, among other things, a champagne bottle and a cell phone. The beating was in response to a disagreement between Puffy and Stoute over a music video.

Puffy originally appeared in the video for the Nas cut "Hate Me Now," which, as implied by the title, is an aggressive response to the haters among us. The video pictures the two figures in a mock crucifixion nailed to their respective crosses, as they rap about the perils of being rich and famous, while so many others want to see them fall. Nas drops this,

> Hate on me/I blew/but I'm the same ole 'G'/people warn me/when you're on top/there's envy/took my niggas out the 'hood/but you doubt on us/Saying' we left the 'hood/but can't get it out of us/my bad/should I step out my shoes/give 'em to you? here are my cars and my house/you can live in that too/criticize when I flow for the streets/hate my dress code/Gucci this/Fendi that/what you expect hoe?

Puffy, upon reflection, decided that the representation could be interpreted as though he was equating himself with Christ and because of this he wanted his image taken out of the video. It was too late, the video was being aired in its original form. For this, Puffy is said to have responded to Stoute with a champagne bottle beating.

It is not completely ironic that Puffy's disagreement with Stoute was over the casting of himself as a martyr figure. Throughout his career Puffy has represented himself as the victim of jealous, vicious playa haters who are intent on seeing him fall off the lofty perch upon which he sits. Thus, the video image could be read as the furthest extension of that martyr pose, and considering the latent and not so latent Christianity that often informs elements of hip hop, this would not be an extension that he would necessarily want to make.

Although P. Diddy has certainly done enough to garner the wrath of a large camp of potential haters, as indicated by websites with names like "The Anti Puffy Daddy Page" or "I Hate Puffy Daddy." I find the at-times-immense ill feelings that he receives within the hip hop community to be rooted in a class riff that still infects large segments of the Black community, not to mention the segments of the White world who have no interest in seeing a Black man with money.

Diddy, to me, is obviously a middle-class Black man who is being forced to define himself against the lower-class standards that dominate hip hop imagery. Hip hop has certainly brought a much-needed class critique to bear on African American culture at large, but it has also been responsible for upping the ante against those Blacks who might happen to be middle class but who remain down with the culture. Much of the contempt against Diddy is generated by the fact that he is proud to declare his love of a lifestyle that many see as outside their realm of experience.

This sentiment is often contrasted against that directed against someone like Tupac, who has been held up as exemplary by many in the hip hop community, including the prominent critical figure Michael Eric Dyson in his book *Holler If You Hear Me: Searching for Tupac Shakur.* Dyson states, "Tupac's ghetto sainthood features all of the elements that render historic figures as embodied presences of divine inspiration. It is surely difficult to trace the anatomy of his spiritual power, though the acclaim he continues to receive from youth across the world is adequate testimony to his enduring significance" (267).

Dyson has consistently and courageously used his widespread media visibility to argue the case of hip hop to mainstream audiences who desperately need to hear this from such an enlightened figure—especially within the conservative elements of the Black church. Still, I would suggest that Dyson's martyrlike celebration of 'Pac in *Holler* is potentially a bit quixotic, though his reading does affirm a dominant sentiment in hip hop regarding the slain figure.

Tupac's mediated image has often been regarded as the essence of realism in contemporary culture. Yet it was most certainly contrived, maybe even more so than any other rap figure. It was contrived in such a way, though, that not only did the hip hop community accept this persona as real but 'Pac started to believe it himself. Tupac's mediated persona and this mediated sense of realism would become the standard by which all others would be measured in the hip hop community. He was successful in convincing people that the image was real, so much so that the fantasy became reality, and at some level, this fantasy would also lead to his real death.

'Pac was a figure who initially gained prominence as an actor, though he would go on to superstardom, primarily by virtue of his music. More than any other rapper, 'Pac, who, though born into a conventional ghetto narrative of poverty and single motherhood, somehow managed to attend a Baltimore performing arts high school, would become a victim of the media because of the visual image first rendered in his performance as the nihilistic Bishop in the 1991 film *Juice*. He would spend the rest of his career trying to live up to that image, while constantly blurring the line between fact and fiction in the process, even in death.

'Pac's lower-class image of "thug life" (the hate you gave little infants fucks everybody), his mediated sense of rage, nihilism, and overall indifference were read as authentic, and it was this mediated sense of the authentic that has come to function as real for many in the hip hop generation. There is now a cottage industry that has grown up around a conspiracy in the aftermath of his death that lies somewhere between Jim Morrison and Elvis Presley.

Unlike his many supporters, though, I find that 'Pac's image is often mistakenly celebrated because his self-destructive nihilism is incorrectly thought to be the authentic expression of all ghetto dwellers and this, of course, is used to cancel out all other possibilities. I have no use for figures who are not interested in moving forward but instead wallow in their self- loathing.

'Pac was never interested in gettin' money, and he certainly was not about gettin' better. He seemed more interested in "stirrin' up shit," as they say, "just for the fuck of it." Puff and Biggie, on the other hand, were about constantly taking the game to higher levels. And though many hip hop heads would have me locked up for invoking Puff here, in relation to 'Pac, a quote from Diddy himself here best sums up my interest in the topic: "I can't help it, I'm an optimist." The fact that Diddy would feel the need to apologize, as it were, signals loud and clear the looming negative influence 'Pac has had on the articulation of the hip hop psyche.

'Pac may be the patron saint of hip hop for many, but for me he was a very good actor who convinced people that he epitomized the "real," yet he was about as constructed a figure as one could imagine.

Bling Bling

The idea of playa hatin' is also seemingly concurrent with another hip hop phenomenon known alternatively as flossin', shinin', or better yet, "bling, bling." All of these have to do with an outward celebration of one's wealth, success, and overall status in life. What in an early generation might have been called "showing off" has now grown into an integral part of self-expression in hip hop circles. The idea of the "come up" represents social mobility in spite of overwhelming obstacles and the politics of this move are deeply embedded in hip hop's master narrative. The expression of this upward mobility by these lower-class individuals, flossin' on one's cars, homes, clothes, money, and lifestyle, has become commonplace. As Biggie often said, "Money, clothes and hoes, all a nigga knows."

Yet one need not assume that this exists only in hip hop, for both Common on his track "A Film Called Pimp" and Michael Eric Dyson in *I May Not Get There with You* astutely point out that the Black preacher, like the rapper and athlete, is another visible figure who stands out for his flamboyance. The Black church regularly features its own version of the playas ball, complete with cats like mega TV preacher T. D. Jakes, who appears dressed as he could have been featured in *American Pimp*. His eight-button double-breasted purple suit with the gold buttons and the matching "gators," his ice, and his multimillion-dollar income place him right in the same vein as Jay-Z, Shaq, and Puffy.

Black preachers, though, tend to escape the scope of the mainstream's wrath, this in spite of the fact that they often possess a great deal of influence over the community. In Los Angeles, for instance, a very popular Black church known as Faithful Central recently purchased the Great Western Forum. The Forum was the home of the Los Angeles Lakers for many years before they moved to the Staples Center in 1999. When filled to its capacity, it holds about seventeen thousand people. This is more than simply the purchase of an arena; it is a statement. The church is saying that its influence is so large, its mandate so strong, that it needs an arena in which to hold services.

The details of this purchase were being worked out while another prominent Black church in Los Angeles, the West Angeles Church of God in Christ, was completing the building of a massive cathedral on the highly visible intersection of Crenshaw Boulevard and Jefferson, an intersection that many African Americans in Los Angeles still consider the main drag into the Black community. It is reported that the new cathedral was being partially financed by large donations from celebrities like Magic Johnson and Denzel Washington. There is a strong Black-celebrity component to the membership of this church, and this is used in the church's efforts to attract new members. If this is not flossin', then nothing is. Yet this will never been seen as flossin', for it feeds a strong desire to see the Black church remain central to the image of the Black community.

In some ways, one could argue that the Black church is ultimately not a threat to any of the larger sources of power in our society; it is a complement.

Though the church's influence reaches a large number of people, its politics of accommodation limits whatever potential impact the institution may have in altering existing power relations. If ever there was a situation in which Black people were being urged to stay in their place, it is the Black church that promotes this thought fully.

The Black church has not only bought into the system but become an integral part of the system itself. The church tends to profit well from the relationship. Black preachers have long had a prominent place in political discussions, and the congregations have always provided a forum for any politicians seeking the Black vote. Thus, the focus on the church as a problematic sort is foreign to most people. A focus on hip hop as problematic, though, goes unquestioned.

At this point in history, the Black church has far too much influence on the affairs of Black people. Its often retrograde message tends to be immune to the sort of criticism that is often leveled against other forms of Black culture. One could even call the church a sacred cow because it often appears to be beyond the criticism that is leveled at other forms of Black cultural expression.

Hip hop certainly has moments when it completely endorses the place of the church in the community. No doubt. This is evident if for no other reason than the ubiquity of the diamond-studded cross that dangles from the necks of so many hip hop artists and followers of the culture. However, there have been moments when hip hop artists have rejected this passive stance in favor of a more varied critique of this unquestioned influence.

Ice Cube does a compelling job of critiquing the influence of the church on his cut "(They Won't Call Me a Nigger) When I Get to Heaven." Using Marvin Gaye's classic "Inner City Blues (Make Me Wanna Holler)" as the background, Cube allows the refrain "make me wanna holler" to echo his frustration with Black people's blind embrace of the church. For instance, he astutely points out the flossin' that often surrounds church attendance, "cause I see/cause I know/the church ain't nothin' but a fashion show."

More important, Ice Cube also connects the church to the racist history of American society, "You're blessed with the Father/Son/and the Holy Ghost/but my whole neighborhood is comatose/lookin' for survival/the devil made you a slave/and he gave you a bible." This connection between racism, White supremacy, and the Black church is often ignored or, worse, rationalized by those who embrace the church as an authentic sign of Blackness. Cube extends the racial connection by suggesting that "the same white man who put me in the slammer/he bombed a church in Alabama," here linking the prison industrial complex with hypocritical religious posturing.

Any influence that goes unchecked has the potential to be damaging to the people who fall under the spell of that influence. The way in which the Black church has functioned relative to influencing the overall culture is such that any criticism of it tends to get negated by a discourse that labels any potential objection to be that of a nonbeliever, a playa hater, in essence. For this reason, Black preachers and other such religious figures have hidden behind the cloth, causing our critical scrutiny to veer toward observing the deeds of others while ignoring the transgressions of the former. Take, for instance, the case of Henry Lyons, the Florida Baptist minister and former head of the National Baptist Convention who was convicted of major financial improprieties; he was encouraged to stay on his post as head of one of the nation's largest Black religious organizations.

This is why people can hold Puffy up to a high moral standard but minimize if not ignore the damage done by these other wolves in pimps' clothing. In the same way, we might potentially miss the acts of power often exhibited by those individuals who have been fortunate enough to exist and influence mainstream culture without having to pay allegiance to the demands of the Black party line in the process. There are those Black figures who appear to be independent of the dictates of this party line and who tend to move with ease through mainstream White society. In my mind, these are the figures who demonstrate some sense of Black power and agency that supersedes the conventional. It is one thing for a president to call on a Black minister in his time of personal crisis, but it is something quite different to see a Black man like Puffy, for instance, reconfigure power in his relationship to White masculinity and by extension, White culture.

There are two examples of Diddy's power that demand our attention. The first took place in the aftermath of the murder of Biggie Smalls. When Puffy began his new record label Bad Boy back in 1994, he dropped tracks by two artists: Craig Mack and the Notorious B.I.G. Though Craig Mack hit with his classic "Flava in Your Ear," he was soon forgotten when Biggie's *Ready to Die* hit the streets. Biggie was destined to be a rap superstar the minute he came on the scene. His clever lyrics, incredible storytelling style, distinct Brooklyn cadence, and overall persona of a big lovable gangsta were somewhere between Barry White, Jackie Gleason, and Sidney Greenstreet. With the aid of Hype Williams's ultraflashy video style, Biggie would become seemingly an overnight star. He contributed guest appearances on a number of other records and by the time of his unnecessary death in 1997, he was arguably the most popular commercial rapper who had managed to maintain a certain street credibility as it were. He was an icon and a symbol of Brooklyn, the East Coast, and ultimately hip hop itself.

When Biggie was gunned down at the Petersen Automotive Museum on that now-infamous corner of Wilshire and Fairfax, it appeared as though Puffy's empire was in ruins. His signature artist was gone, and Puffy had effectively used Biggie to help publicize his lesser artists, and now this too was no longer an option. Biggie's album dropped shortly after his murder and went on to dominate the charts and people's minds for some time. Yet what was the next step?

Puffy, pressed for answers, turned to the only person he knew he could count on: himself. In the summer of 1997, Puff Daddy's *No Way Out* was released with the shadow and voice of Biggie still assuming a prominent place on the record and in association with Puffy as well. The album was dedicated to the memory of B.I.G. and featured a few tributes to the fallen artist, most notably, "I'll Be Missing You," which gave prominence to an interpolation of the great Police song with Sting's distinct vocals, "Every Breath You Take." Puffy surprised everyone when Sting appeared with him at the MTV Awards singing the chorus himself.

The symbolism of this moment cannot be lost. Puffy first of all had angered a number of people throughout the hip hop community by sampling so many popular songs, many of them by White artists like The Police or David Bowie. There is an unspoken creed in hip hop that seems to suggest that sampling of any popular songs is bad and sampling pop songs from White acts is, as Curtis Mayfield would say, "worser." Similar to the way that MC Hammer had once appropriated the popular Rick James song "Super Freak," Puff had now housed the Sting track with no shame.

Production in hip hop favors originality. It is thought that the best producers, like Premiere, RZA, Dr. Dre, or Jay Dee, for example, are those who though they may use samples and break beats, do so in such a way as to disguise masterfully their origin and reinterpret their meaning in the process of the song. To the extent that someone uses an obvious reference, it is often done for ironic purposes. Thus to pull an obvious record like "Every Breath You Take," a song whose MTV video was certainly one of the most prevalent for its time, and to play this seriously was considered such an overt attempt at pop stardom that it was thought shameful.

To make matters worse, Puffy early on tended to display some undeveloped lyrical skills and a repetitive rhyme scheme that many would call "wack." Yet in spite of this, he would come to dominate the charts and increasingly he would come to dominate the public image of hip hop. Many forget or at least work to revise history because Tupac, in his early days was quite unimpressive as a rapper too, but eventually his powerful image would come to elevate what people thought of his actual skills as a rapper.

Lyrical skills notwithstanding, Puffy's status as a mogul within the industry gives him a certain luxury that few others can claim. On the track "Bad Boy for Life," he declares, "[D]on't worry if I write rhymes/I write checks." Here, he underscores the bottom line. Lyrical skills may be the standard by which fans judge the music, but it is Puffy's bankroll that truly distinguishes him from those who simply perform.

The resentment toward Puffy's sudden ubiquity, in a culture that emphasizes authenticity at all costs, can best be heard on the Wu Tang introduction of side 2 of their 1997 album *Triumph*. The words of RZA here were like the throwing down of the gauntlet. Realness was being questioned. Could hip hop be popular and retain its hard-core edge? Puffy was at the center of the debate. His history had hard core written all over it, but his claim to Biggie's legacy was in serious question the more popular he became.

RZA declares his heartfelt sentiment, and this to me has become like a call to arms, a hip hop manifesto like none other.

> I wanna give y'all a lil' announcement. For the last year there's been a lot of music comin' out and that shit's been weak.
>
> Knowhatl'msayin', lot of niggaz try to take hip-hop and make that shit R&B, rap 'n bullshit, knowwhatl'msayin', or make that shit funk. Fuck that! This is MCin', right here, this is hip hop. The Wu Tang is gonna bring it to ya in the purest form.

RZA begins his statement by declaring his immediate intentions for this to serve as a statement of purpose. He suggests that hip hop should continue to distinguish itself from R&B, which is thought to be most commercial, and at some level, in the hypermasculine perceptions of hip hop, intended for feminine taste. Not stopping there, RZA also indicts funk, which though masculine would still be considered too overdetermined by danceable beats. His suggestion of purity, the purest form, calls attention to the corrupting influences of the mainstream, while highlighting hip hop's quest for authenticity:

> This ain't no R&B with a wack nigga takin' a loop. Be loopin' that shit, thinkin' it's gonna be, the sound of the culture, know what I'm sayin'. Or

all that player dressin' up. . . . act like this is a fashion show man, knowwhatI'msayin'. This is hip-hop right here, knowwhatI'msayin'. This is lyrics, MCin'. And yo, ya'll niggaz who think you goin' become an MC overnight, yaknowwhatI'msayin, better snap out that fuckin' dream. It takes years for this. Cat-in-the-hat-ass rappers. You Dr. Seuss–Mother Goose simple-minded . . . niggaz ain't made for this, knowwhatI'msayin'. This shit was only built for cuban links!

Many rappers began to use Puffy as the artist they most defined themselves against. His emphasis on dance music for the clubs and the consciously over-the-top Hype Williams' videos, which foregrounded, among other things, Puffy's shiny suits, began to make many feel that Puffy was betraying the hard-core image of the man who had brought his label fame in the first place, Biggie.

P. Diddy acknowledges this critique while making light of himself on his new disc, produced under the name P. Diddy and the Bad Boy Family and called *The Saga Continues* (2001). Here he uses a humorous skit entitled "The Shiny Suit Man" that both recognizes and deflates his own self-important persona. Puffy was, like B.I.G., trying to curry favor with the club set and the streets at the same time, but very few rappers, with the notable exception of someone like Jay-Z, are able to do such a thing, then or now, which is really a testament to B.I.G.'s influence on the game.

At some point, people began to assume that any pop success was automatically suspect, and this, of course, denies any possibility of ever transcending the historical limits that hinder racial and cultural progress. If no one can ever transcend the limits of the past, then what is the point? If we accept this, then there is no reason to live, for one's life and place in the world is already determined. This defeatist attitude is a self-fulfilling prophecy.

This is not to suggest, however, that there are not many racial, social, and political obstacles to overcome, nor does it suggest that any of this will be easily accomplished. Instead, the road to success, social mobility, and in some ways, self-determination is fraught with various hurdles that make the journey itself difficult but also make for a triumphant feeling when one does finally succeed, against all odds. The idea of surviving, of overcoming seemingly insurmountable odds, is at the core of Black existence in America, and has been fine-tuned through a number of contemporary examples of culture.

Although some are like Tupac, who seemed to accept his fate, even wallow in it, this while celebrating the predictions of his own death, others are like Puffy, who chooses to live and fight on. This battle with the powers that be, with the haters of society, is a constant struggle, and when one does make it, on one's own terms, it is cause for celebration. This is why so many Black athletes attract the ire of the mainstream when they openly celebrate their accomplishments. Mainstream White social decorum suggests that one be humble and unassuming. This is fine when you control everything and there is no need to be visible. It is another issue entirely when you have nothing and are constantly trying to be seen and heard. Each little step along the way is a victory, especially when it is already determined that you will lose, before you even start the game.

When one considers that the people in question are often from lower-class backgrounds, this celebration is one that also expresses a political point, one that says in spite of all the obstacles imposed by a racist society, the individual in question has, at least momentarily, been successful. Yet, when one considers the power dynamic in America, it is often the case that those who have come up, as it were, are on top only for a second, a relatively short-lived success, ensured by the fact that the individuals in question have little to no experience dealing with wealth and the incumbent demands on managing one's money. Therefore, a story like the financial rise and fall of someone like Hammer, becomes fodder for a VH1 "Behind the Music" documentary.

What happens when you are a middle-class African American, like Puff, who, having some, albeit limited, exposure to the workings of moneyed White America, comes up? In other words, it is apparent to anyone looking objectively that Puffy is not simply another ghetto ass nigga, in spite of how ghetto fabulous he might try to act sometimes.

What has been most interesting about the P. Diddy affect is that he has managed to break into elements of wealthy White society that would normally be off-limits to most other Black people, and especially off-limits to other ghetto-defined rappers. Though Def Jam mogul Russell Simmons has long been a fixture in the elite White world of celebrity and influence, Russell's somewhat humble by contrast presence was never as visible. Puff, on the other hand, has received a great deal of publicity for, among other things, his house in the Hamptons and his circle of prominent White associates. Yet, instead of its appearing that Puffy wanted to be included in this mix, he was seen as the one whom others wanted to be next to.

In a much-talked-about Hamptons summer "White" party, Puff here reworks the imagery once made famous by Truman Capote's Black and White Ball. Puff had a guest list that included the likes of prominent mainstream White figures such as Martha Stewart and Donald Trump, figures thought to be far removed from the hip hop milieu. One guest, Ronald O. Perlman, the owner of Revlon, was said to have arrived at the party dressed in something other than the required White attire. It is said that Perlman was refused entry, upon which he left, only to return wearing the appropriate attire.

Although this may be insignificant to some, it is an instance of power and a representation of the changing times as well. When a revered leader of industry like Perlman finds it necessary to change his clothes in order to attend a party in a White wealthy enclave like the Hamptons because a Black man said so, it is a sign that Puff's power, presence, and image are something to be respected. The symbolism of the White clothes is not lost either.

Something similar was at work again when Puffy threw a lavish birthday party for himself at a New York restaurant, Cipriani's, in 1999. Puffy made the who who's of his guest list wait several hours before he finally arrived. Now, some may balk at this as nothing other than Puffy's arrogance, but it is indicative of something much more powerful. Puffy is saying, simply, "Wait on me, muthafucka, this is my party and you want to be here so bad because I am the hippest nigga on the planet right now." Puff recognizes his power as that of a style and taste arbiter. He is in New York, after all, a place not short on celebrity power, but his status is even on top of that.

In calling himself the "Black Sinatra," Puffy is saying that he has the same sort of appeal, status, and importance as that legendary White icon of another era, Frank Sinatra. When he declares on "Let's Get It" that "my name is Diddy/I run this city/send the cops/the feds/the DA/to come get me," he is not only castigating those who tried to bring him down in the courtroom but also celebrating the money, power, and respect that he has been able to achieve through culture. It is his undeniable determination, his undying quest for legendary status that propels his ascension.

As implied by titles such as "Can't Nobody Hold Me Down" or the Biggie track "Sky's the Limit" and the hook from "Bad Boy for Life" which declares, "[W]e ain't/goin'/nowhere/we ain't/goin' nowhere/we can't be stopped now/cause it's Bad Boy for life," it is obvious that Puffy will not be denied. This determination is not unlike that which has made so many Black athletes superstars of their respective sports, a determination that is underscored by the looming presence of defeat that society has already prescribed. When one watches an Allen Iverson play basketball, for instance, it is apparent that he may be the smallest man on the court, but his refusal to accept this fate makes him so intoxicating to watch. In spite of this overwhelming size disadvantage, in a game defined by height, Iverson manages to succeed, and he does so on his own terms. This is in many ways the definition of desire at the highest level.

Though Puff may not be the best rapper, his desire, his refusal not to let that admitted shortcoming stop him, is equally impressive. When you factor this into his overall business empire, his Sean John clothing line, his Harlem Kingpin status, he is that much more impressive. There has always been a politics of pleasure to Puffy's persona that make many, even in the hip hop community, uncomfortable. Remember, a Black is not supposed to have any fun, and of course should never smile. Puffy defies all this, and it is truly empowering to watch him live out his life in such a dramatic fashion. He, in some ways, has the last laugh.

Creepin' on a Come Up

> I come up hard/but now I'm cool/I didn't make it/baby/playing by the rules.
> . . . I come up hard/I had to fight/took care my bidness/with all my might/I come up hard/I had to win/then start all over/and win again.
>
> —Marvin Gaye, "Trouble Man"

Cultural movements tend to start as their own entities. Hip hop is no different. In the celebrated early days of hip hop, this new form of cultural expression grew out of the conditions of the time. No one sat down and said, "I'm going to create hip hop." They simply did it. This was not a conscious move but, instead, a direct action. For many, this is a time of innocence, and because of this, we celebrate the moment as one of purity. We somehow assume that because there was no conscious thought about manipulating the direction of the music then, that it is somehow more noble in its intentions than later in their career when people recognize the market potential and want to sell records along with making an artistic statement.

Hip hop is defined by a strong sense of historical identity. The phrase "back in the day" connotes this at a high level. There is a celebration of history. From the acknowledgments or "shout outs" to old school rappers, the sampling of old music, or the wearing of old school fashion, hip hop is all about history. Often this history provides a vehicle for the articulation of one's autobiography, and in this there is a narrative trajectory that has to do with starting off at one point and eventually getting to another higher point. Biggie Smalls's *Ready to Die* represents the canonical text in regard to expressing this history and linking it to a certain social mobility.

This positive arch in one's life is referred to as "the come up" and has been expressed through several memorable hip hop phrases, which include, among others, Biggie's famous statements "I went from ashy to classy," or "from ten keys of blow/to thirty g's a show/to orgies with hoes I never seen before"; Nas's use of the timepiece to imply that he went from "from Seiko to Rolex"; or Common's journey from "bashful to asshole to international." In each case, the rapper's move from one point to the next, from low to high, from poverty to wealth is used to demonstrate this notion of the come up and identifies one's struggle to achieve success.

Other artists have also used the past as a way of painting a vivid picture that functions much like a lyrical photo album, where well-known icons from a formative period serve to accentuate the artist's place in the present moment. Talib Kweli references this sense on the title to his debut album *Train of Thought* (2000), recorded with his partner DJ Hi Tek and working under the group name Reflection Eternal. Talib underscores this hip hop historicism on a track titled simply "Memories Live":

> Know it kinda make me think of way back when/I was the portrait of an
> artist as a young man/all them teenage dreams of rappin'/writin' rhymes on
> napkins/it was really visualization/makin' this here actually happen/it's like
> something comin' through me/that truly just consumes me/speaks through
> the voice of spirits/speaking to me/I say back in the day/I absorb everything
> like a sponge/took a plunge into my past/to share with my son.

"Memories Live" uses as its hook a bit of the chorus from a famous 1973 Ann Peebles song "I Can't Stand the Rain." The words "bringin' back sweet memories" echo throughout the Kweli track to enhance this sense of nostalgia. Kweli here uses this sense of history to describe his own ascendancy, while linking this to the craft of hip hop, concluding it with a present-day connection to his "seed," and at the same time positing this historicism for a future generation. His invocation of James Joyce is well taken as he moves from one point, concluding in another, and rein-scribing hip hop's straightforward narrative progress in the process.

This sense of history breeds a heightened nostalgia, which forms a romanti-cized link to the past. Hip hop certainly has its romantic side as this love of the "old school" firmly expresses the culture's connection to its history. As a result of this embrace of the nostalgic, though, there is often a concurrent response that has come to be articulated as a decline narrative that regards the historical as the most authentic and often foregrounds one's early efforts as the best example of one's work. This too has often underlined this sense of hatin' in regard to artists becom-ing more popular. Even now, the artists who tend to receive praise in hip hop cir-cles are those who "take it back."

I'm the N to A to the S-I-R/If I wasn't/I musta been Escobar.

—Nas, "You're the Man"

A good example of this tendency to embrace history at the cost of all else can be found in the career pattern traveled by hip hop stalwart Nas. When the son of mu-sician Olu Dare, Nasir Jones, aka Nas, appeared on the hip hop landscape in the early 1990s it was as though a new child prodigy had just entered the room. When Nas's first album, *Illmatic,* was released in 1994, it struck a chord with many hip hop heads. This was during the height of West Coast dominance in hip hop and several people had begun to write off the East Coast, the original birthplace of hip hop, as having faded into oblivion. Jay-Z most accurately sums up this period in a memorable line from his track "This Can't Be Life" when he states, "[I]t's like '93/'94/when Big and Mack dropped/and *Illmatic* rocked/out of every rag drop/and the west had it locked." The West Coast dominance of Dr. Dre and Snoop during this time had made the East Coast secondary until Puff dropped both the Mack and B.I.G. discs around the same time that Nas's first record came out. These records indicated that the East Coast was still viable as a style and foreshadowed the dominance that it would reclaim some years later.

Illmatic is a hip hop classic of the first order. Nas's poetic lyrics are some of the most poignant words ever to describe the postindustrial urban experience. His spoken-wordlike delivery and his vivid use of metaphor placed him at the top of the game in terms of his overall skills as an MC and as a cultural commentator. The baby-faced Nas was a young man blessed with a old spirit when *Illmatic* hit the streets and therefore his prescient words had that much more of an impact.

Songs like "Life's a Bitch (And Then You Die)," "It Ain't Hard to Tell," and "The World Is Mine" will be forever be held up as hip hop standard-bearers. Lyrics like "I woke up early on my born day/I'm 20/it's a blessin'/the essence of adolescence/leave my body/now I'm fresh and/my physical frame is celebrated/cause I made it" or "I sip the Dom P/watchin' Ghandi/'til I'm charged/writin' in my book of rhymes/all the words/past the margins" still bring a certain mist to the eyes. As a demonstration of his range of influences, Nas even references Shakespeare when he says on "New York State of Mind," "[I]t drops deep/deep as it does in my breathe/I never sleep/cause sleep is the cousin of death." Nas, in his ability to provide an astute and well-observed portrait of ghetto life from an informed perspective, was a sign that there was still life east of the Mississippi.

On *Illmatic,* Nas often referred to himself as Nasty Nas. This would change, though, with the release of his second album, *It Is Written,* in 1996. Here Nas begins to refer to himself as Nas Escobar, making a very direct connection to the image of super dope dealer Pablo Escobar and insinuating himself with the gangsta clique. In addition, the first single from the album was a duet with Lauryn Hill, whose career was just taking off with The Fugees. The song "If I Ruled the World" featured an elaborate video, and the presence of Hill gave it a potential R&B feel.

This proved to be anathema to many who had embraced the phenom on his first record. Many felt that Nas had abandoned his roots in the streets and was instead now seeking only pop stardom.

Shortly thereafter, Nas, AZ, and Foxy Brown would record a concept album with Dr. Dre under the name The Firm. Though the record contained one of the greatest hip hop beats ever from the track of a song called "Phone Tap," it was routinely dismissed as another crass example of the pursuit of pop stardom at the expensive of true hip hop artistry. When Nas released *I Am* and *Nastradamus* in 1999, he was almost completely ignored if not begrudged by those who had once held him up as a true hip hop soldier of the highest rank.

Nas's decline even became the impetus behind one of hip hop's greatest battle raps to date, when Jay-Z spelled all this out in his combative track "The Takeover" from his 2001 classic *The Blueprint*, going so far as to say, in reference to Nas, that "you started out with a spark/but now you're just garbage/went from top ten/to not mentioned at all."

This is a classic example of the decline narrative at work in hip hop culture and the hate that it engenders in the process. The move from Nasty Nas, to Nas Escobar, to Nastradamus, is thought by many to be a decline indicative of what happens when one lets dollars dictate one's art, as opposed to passion. Many even see the latter efforts as a betrayal of Nas's original statement. This, I think, is somewhat problematic.

Though *Illmatic* is without a doubt one of the most important chapters in hip hop, the other records reveal equally strong statements. There is the amazing "I Gave You Power," which speaks about a view of the world, with the narrator's assuming the perspective of a gun, and the great tribute song to Tupac and Biggie "We Will Survive," not to mention one of the illest narratives ever put on record in the overlooked track "Undying Love." To dismiss Nas now is like assuming that because Shaquille O'Neal no longer breaks backboards that he is no longer a good basketball player. This is ridiculous.

People have been unable to accept Nas in transition, and they assume that whatever he said at one point he should continue to say forever. There is a problem here with this because it does not allow Nas or hip hop, for that matter, to grow. This idea says that hip hop is forever confined to its own history in a prison-like relationship. Why would we expect a young man evolving through his formative years to remain at the same place, while the world around him is constantly changing? If Nas is still rapping about the same thing, six or seven years later, then, he might be keepin' it real, as some suspect, but in reality, he has made no progress.

These narratives of decline do not allow for growth but, instead, insist on a locked and immovable position, an attitude that can in no way produce anything fruitful. In my mind, there is a constant tension between the personas of Nasty Nas, Nas Escobar, and Nastradamus, and this tension is to be expected in a world where our identity is constantly being split along this postmodern axis. Yet many are unable to accept this tension and instead see it as a contradiction, assuming, however incorrectly, that there is a original authentic self that has been corrupted rather than recognizing how these various representations of the self are natural points of evolution that work to expose the challenges toward a creative impulse.

Nas, though, bolstered by all this, went back to the drawing board and dropped *Stillmatic* at the end of 2001 and, in doing so, not only responded to Jay-Z's taunts but also demonstrated that he was still relevant, and could still lay claim to being one of the greatest hip hop poets ever. In the aftermath of the murders of Tupac Shakur and the great Biggie Smalls, hip hop had, for the most part, avoided direct confrontations like the one that led to these untimely deaths. It was clear when listening to Tupac rant and rave like a demented fool on the single "Hit 'Em Up" that this war of words, between East and West, had gone much too far. The imaginary line that we Black folks know all too well had been crossed.

It's like back in the day when we used to play the dozens, everybody knew when the line had been crossed and someone started taking offense to what was originally a joke and began to take it seriously, when someone had hit a nerve and things were on their way to getting out of hand. This is when you knew if you kept going, you would eventually have to squab. Well, Tupac went too far, talkin' about niggas having sickle cell, and fuckin' someone's wife, and before you knew it, two more young Black men had gotten capped, way before their time.

Well, in the aftermath of such a sorrowful series of events, hip hop had become a kinder, gentler nation, one content on making money, driving Bentleys, drinking expensive Cristal champagne, wearing platinum jewelry, and, for all intents and purposes, not givin' a fuck. Then, almost like a sign, on September 11, Jay-Z's sixth album, *The Blueprint*, dropped and hip hop's sleeping dogs woke up. The second track on *The Blueprint* was a tune called "The Takeover," which in addition to its clever Jim Morrison sample, directly targeted both Nas and his Queensbridge homie Prodigy of the group Mobb Deep. The gloves were off, and Jay was goin' for his. The track ignited a long-held hip hop tradition, that of the battle rap. A tradition that had been dormant in the aftermath of the 'Pac/Biggie scenario. Like the cuttin' sessions of old, or the battle of the bands, the battle rap represents hip hop's contemporary take on the competitive nature embedded in the oral expression of the culture. When done properly, the competition feeds on itself, and often the creative result is a masterpiece. Imagine the competition of a great NBA game and then transform it into music. As Jay-Z himself said during his performance on MTV's *Unplugged* in late 2001, the battle rap is in keeping with "the truest essence of hip hop." Yes, the battle is a genuine war of words, indeed.

Jay-Z's diss of Nas was such that it forced Nas to respond, which he did on his album *Stillmatic*, with the track "Ether." As long as the competition remains confined to the lyrics, everything will be just fine, and there is no reason to assume otherwise. Both Jay-Z and Nas have too much money and too much at stake to throw it away on some bullshit, the obvious lessons learned from 'Pac and Biggie notwitstanding. Hey, as Nas himself even said, "[T]he best always clash at the top." So there it is.

· · ·

News of Nas's demise appears to have been greatly exaggerated. *Stillmatic* even received the prestigious acknowledgment of "five mics" from *The Source* magazine, the highest honor that this hip hop voice of record bestows on any artist. The evolution demonstrates Nas coming full circle and also reveals that it is the whole journey that one must evaluate, not only the small steps along the way. *Stillmatic* would not have been so well received if the albums before it had not been considered such a drop-off from the original *Illmatic*.

This sense of the decline narrative is also something furthered by the music industry as it tries to sell more and more product. In the past, there was much more emphasis put into truly developing an artist. An artist's first record was not intended to be his or her greatest career output but, instead, the beginning of the journey. An artist might make several records and have to change record labels before finding the right combination to produce a hit. Think about Aretha Franklin's early unnoticed work on the Columbia label before going to icon status later on when she signed with Atlantic Records. Or one might reference the early incarnation of George Clinton as a suit-and-tie doo wop clone of The Temptations with a group called The Parliaments signed to the Motown label. This was quite different from the space age funk Clinton later became known for on the Casablanca label with his group Parliament Funkadelic. Though if it happened it would be welcomed, no one expected an artist's first album to be great right off the bat. The artist, like the examples above, had an opportunity to grow into something, instead of being expected to be that something right off.

This, of course, was in the days before music videos had such an influence on an artist's success. Now, the music industry regularly markets "one-hit wonders," putting all the eggs in one basket, and often dropping the act in question if it does not hit immediately. This is not simply nostalgia for a different era, either; it is more a commentary on the modern music industry and the way in which its marketing strategies influence consumer tastes. If an artist is to truly have an impact, he or she must create a body of work. This is how something should be judged: by the body of work, not by a single work.

The first album is also the one whereby the industry stands to make the most money, in that the artist is at a disadvantage, with little to no leverage until he or she has a proven track record for moving units. In addition, most artists come into the game ignorant of way that the industry does business. For instance, most people outside the industry do not know that the cost of making a music video comes from an advance on the artist's contract. When the record is released, the money fronted for the video must be recouped before any profits will be extended to the artist. Therefore, if one has a million-dollar video, one is already in the hole, not to mention the money for studio time and related expenses that are charged back against the artist. There is no way a young artist off the street can have any idea of how this works before being introduced to it through an initial music industry experience.

Record industry contracts are based on previous units sold, so any artist coming in has to establish a track record before he or she can claim to have any real leverage. For this reason, the first standard contract often reflects this lack of experience, and the artist must then prove him or herself a viable record seller before demanding any real stake in the proceeds.

One of the areas where many artists truly get beat is publishing. The ownership of one's songwriting copyright, or publishing, is potentially the most valuable resource, for the proprietor receives money forever, whenever someone else is interested in playing and using the material in question. Publishing deals pay out royalty money long after the record is off the shelf. Yet many unseasoned artists have no idea of this and are generally victimized because of it in the process.

There are many legendary stories of rappers and other artists being beat out of their royalties, going back to the authors of all those classic blues songs who never got credit for their work to more contemporary figures like The D.O.C., who was said to have sold his publishing to the late Easy E for "a watch and a chain" one day while strolling through an LA area mall.

I must also point out that not all hip hop figures are unaware of the money game. Many people in hip hop have had extensive dealings in the dope world, thus their knowledge of ownership rights and money management is, in this regard, quite sophisticated. It is also for this reason that many hip hop figures now own their master recordings, which is something unheard of in the music business. The ownership of the master recordings means that one controls any future use of the recordings and participates in any future profits. Record companies have long used their ownership of master recordings to make money well after a record has receded from public consciousness. Well, because many in hip hop have the experience of handling large sums of dope loot and the volatility that goes along with making money in that profession, they are potentially less susceptible to being bilked of their profits.

New Orleans mogul Master P, for instance, made a great deal of money selling his music independently, concentrating on the southern regional market around his native New Orleans. After his phenomenal success down South many of the major record labels began courting P, who, in turn balked at the initial offers he received for the standard 85 percent to 15 percent share that favors the record distributors over the actual independent record label. P was used to getting all the profit when selling his records in the low key regional manner in which he had already excelled. Why should he now accept only 15 percent when he had been getting 100 percent? Thus, he was ultimately able to negotiate a more favorable deal for himself and his No Limit operation.

Though many people feel that Black entertainers, or Black people in general for that matter, do not know how to manage money, examples like that of Master P, someone who wears gold fronts in his mouth and is not thought to be intelligent by mainstream standards, clearly demonstrate the way that these racist perceptions are completely unfounded.

Yet, there are still the others whose relative inexperience in the music industry makes it easier for them to come in at a financial disadvantage. For all these reasons, artists are easy to manipulate because the record label has smaller expenses on the front end and thus, if the label does get a hit, its profit margin will be generous. The public tends to oblige here, having been duped into placing all of its interest in the first record and automatically becoming suspicious upon the release of subsequent records.

In this regard, I find the Wu Tang Clan to be representative as one of the few hip hop acts to have had the chance to evolve and thus get better over time. The Wu released their first album, *Enter the Wu Tang (36 Chambers)* in 1993. Like Nas, the Wu Tang were a bit overshadowed by the cacophony of the West Coast gangstas who were dominating at the time. Upon reflection, though, the record opened the way for a whole new style.

The Wu Tang, which merge the imagery of kung fu cinema with a latent Five Percent Nation political sensibility, and a Staten Island or "Shoalin" gangsta pose comprise several members and affiliates, with nine principal members holding down the fort. These include RZA, GZA, Method Man, Ghostface Killah, Raekwon, U God, Cappadonna, Masta Killa, and the now-infamous Old Dirty Bastard, whose name references the fact that "ain't no father to his style." Each rapper also has multiple identities that suggest a sense of being particularly conscious of the demands of a postmodern world. These identities include Bobby Digital(RZA), John Blaze or Hot Nickels(Method Man), Toney Starks (Ghostface), the Chef (Raekwon), and the funniest of all, Osirus or better yet, Big Baby Jesus (Old Dirty). Here, the Clan recognize that the more options available to one as a Black man, the fewer the opportunities to shut one down. RZA provides the beats and musical direction, and all nine of them take turns rapping. The Clan's energy is like that of the Duke Ellington orchestra or Parliament Funkadelic, where the multiple members ply their own unique trade in the context of the larger group.

With the release of *36 Chambers,* RZA laid down his unique minimalist sound and the others stepped to the mic to do their thing, one right after the other. It was like a lyrical onslaught. After the successful release of this record, each of the individual members released solo records, often featuring guest appearances by some of the other Clan members. When they came back to record their second album together, *Triumph,* released in 1997, the results were, as they even admit now, less than spectacular, the title track and its famous "Killer Bees" video notwithstanding. More solo records would follow, and RZA sharpened his Wu sword. RZA, who in my mind, is like the Philip Glass of hip hop, would emerge to drop some of the most sophisticated beats ever and in so doing, distinguish his work and the Clan's from all other rappers. They have a distinct sound that truthfully has no peer.

RZA released his solo record *Bobby Digital* in 1998, and this led to several other outstanding records. His work on Method Man and Redman's *Blackout,* Ghostface Killah's *Supreme Clientele,* the soundtrack for the film *Ghostdog,* and The Wu Tang Clan's third album, *The W,* all released in 1999–2000, represent a collective body of work that few in the hip hop game can ever be said to rival. It is as though all this time together and apart allowed each of the members to sharpen his sword. When they came back together for *The W,* having had a chance to grow and develop, the collective was now greatly enhanced by the sums of its parts.

The Wu Tang Clan are like a great basketball team here, in which there were few real superstars but, instead, a group of very talented individual players who know their roles and who perform these roles to perfection. The team runs nine deep and like the last great NBA *team* to feature more than a few superstars, the Detroit Pistons of the late 1980s and early 1990s, the Wu can destroy with their critical mass. Their creative journey is one seldom seen anymore, though, in a music culture geared to producing one-hit wonders and an audience eager to dispose of its culture, as if it were a McDonald's hamburger wrapper.

Hip Hop on Top

Finally we made it good/hip hop took it to billions/I knew we would.

—Nas, "We Will Survive"

How do we define *progress* in a genre where progress is often looked upon suspiciously? This is the question faced by hip hop now that it has become a lucrative cultural entity permanently etched into the ledger of Americana. How does a culture that started off on the margins deal with its own now-mainstream success? How does hip hop continue to exist in light of all the changes? Has hip hop at times been guilty of hatin' on itself?

Hip hop must now learn to deal with its success and this might prove to be more difficult than dealing with failure. It is sometimes easier to get on top than it is to stay on top. If hip hop were still a completely underground project, if it were still lampoon', if beats were still basic, rhymes basic, lyrics and themes basic, would it have saturated the world in the way that it has now? No. Obviously not.

If the culture is to be responsive to history, as history changes, so then does hip hop. In other words, change is not a bad thing. One cannot be locked into any history that will not allow for growth. Outkast released their fourth album, *Stankonia,* in the fall of 2000. The sound of this record was unlike any other ever released in hip hop. For instance, the first single off the album, "Bombs over Baghdad," features a beat located somewhere between techno, electronica, drum and bass, two step, and southern bounce, which eventually morphs into a gospel choir groovin' on a hip hop tip. The sonic force behind this song was such that it just blew the listener away.

What is important here is that Outkast, refusing to accept another worn-out beat, took a chance, one that surely paid off, financially and also creatively. This move and others like it should be celebrated, as opposed to being dismissed, or else hip hop will die a slow and boring death.

Rawkus Records is a label that specializes in a certain style of conscious hip hop, featuring artists like Mos Def, Kweli, and Pharoah Monch, not to mention reviving the career of an old school underground legend like Kool G Rap. Should Rawkus be ashamed that its label has now become popular and that it is starting to sell a large number of records? Should someone like Common be critiqued because he allows his image to be used in a prominent Reebok ad? Obviously, the answer is no, on all counts. This exposure helps to sell records, and this in turn allows the artists more of an opportunity to sell their respective messages.

One cannot be so locked into a history that one becomes a prisoner to it. Change in status, be it financial, cultural, or political, is not always the worst thing in the world, nor should it be. Actually, it represents progression. Change is at the heart of creativity, and that should be embraced while one maintains a solid understanding of the history that proceeds it. This is not to advocate change for the sake of change but to suggest that change and an understanding of one's history do not have to be mutually exclusive. The two can be simultaneously empowering.

4 Head Nigga in Charge

Slick Willie, Slim Shady, and the Return of the "White Negro"

White skin notwithstanding, this [Bill Clinton] is our first Black president.

—Toni Morrison

Chris Tucker came to my office today. He told me he was playing the first black president. And I said, I've already beat you to the punch: I am the first Black president.

—Bill Clinton speaking to the Congressional Black Caucus

(quoted in the *New York Times*)

William Jefferson Clinton, a gentleman more affectionately known as "Slick Willie," a true hip hop moniker if ever there was one, was simply an aspiring presidential candidate from Hope, Arkansas, when he stepped on the bandstand of *The Arsenio Hall Show* in the spring of 1992 and made history. Sitting in with the band that evening, Clinton, donning dark sunglasses, picked up his "ax" and started riffing on Elvis Presley's classic "Heartbreak Hotel," with as much soul as any White person, even Elvis, had ever exhibited before in public life. Clinton's image, his presidential persona, and, most important, his close connection to the tropes of Blackness and Black people would forever be linked with this appearance on *Arsenio*.

They Ask Me If I Liked Arsenio . . .

Arsenio Hall, the young African American host of the show, had done what was said to be impossible at the time. He had created a late-night talk show that could coexist with the reigning king of late-night television, Johnny Carson. Many had tried before Arsenio, but none of them had been successful. Carson was such a television icon to a particular generation that most would not dare challenge his reign for fear that they would go the way of so many others before. Yet, Arsenio ignored the naysayers and went on to establish his presence as the anti-Carson, the alternative to Carson's unrivaled, though generationally specific, appeal.

Carson was a Cold War phenomenon, and his audience was the generation that Tom Brokaw has described as the "greatest generation." Similar to the sympathetic portrayal evoked by Steven Spielberg in *Saving Private Ryan* (1998), Spielberg's HBO collaboration with Tom Hanks on *Band of Brothers* (which conspicuously omits any Brothas), and Michael Bay's *Pearl Harbor* (2001), Carson's implied audience was those for whom World War II served as the most important historical touchstone.

Arsenio Hall, unlike Carson, was an African American who had come of age in what I have often referred to as the post–civil rights era. Understandably so, his style was also quite different from Carson's. Hall would bound out on the stage nightly, pumping his fist, barking, giving high fives to an audience section known as the "Dawg Pound," wearing colorful double-breasted suits or even more colorful leather jackets, speaking the latest slang, and sporting a trendy high-top fade haircut. This, of course, was the direct opposite of Carson's conservative blazers, slacks, and fake golf swings, not only in style but also in terms of the cultural connections suggested by such specific behavior.

Carson always joked about ultrasuburban "beautiful downtown Burbank"; Arsenio's studio announcer would declare, nightly, that *The Arsenio Hall Show* was where "Hollywood meets the 'Hood." The guests on *Arsenio* furthered this claim. Hall regularly featured rising young African American stars, musical artists, and professional athletes who probably would not have been admitted to Carson's audience, much less been booked to appear on his show. Hall even went so far as to book controversial Nation of Islam leader Louis Farrakhan as a guest on one of his final shows.

In other words, *The Arsenio Hall Show* made no secret of its roots in Black culture, its appeal to the youthful members of this audience, and its connection to the world of hip hop. And, similar to the way that Black culture has functioned in light of American culture historically, *The Arsenio Hall Show,* though *Black*, had a large young White following as well.

To appear on *Arsenio,* then, was a way for Bill Clinton to make a statement. Considering the history of race in America, this could not be avoided. Most traditional politicians would never even consider appealing to this young Black-oriented audience, yet Clinton not only attempted to appeal to this audience but also demonstrated an unusual ease in the environment. Clinton's appearance can now be seen as the initial public declaration regarding his embrace of Black culture, an image that would be amplified throughout his presidency. Again, this public declaration would forever posit the man as sympathetic to Black culture, and by extension, sympathetic to Black people.

This is not unlike Clinton's successful appearance on MTV during this same presidential campaign when he played along and answered a humorous question from a young woman about whether he wore boxers or briefs. In these cases, Clinton demonstrated a comfort level with Black culture, youth culture, and popular culture in general, all three cultural areas that would otherwise suggest something very nonpresidential.

I am convinced that Clinton's appeal to the constituencies implied in these cultural forums made the difference for him in a relatively close three-way election that fall. When you consider that Ronald Reagan kicked off his 1980 presidential campaign in Pulaski, Tennessee, the birthplace of the Ku Klux Klan, Clinton's appearance on *Arsenio,* some twelve years later, offered the direct opposite as a symbolic example. The fact that Clinton would go on to unseat Reagan's partner in crime, George Bush, in the 1992 election, extends this point even further.

What made Clinton such a big hit that night on *Arsenio* was that he broke with the stodgy, officious, formal, read "White," appearance of what is expected of a president. To the extent that masculinity and femininity are also coded specifically by issues of race, class, and sexuality, it is in the president, the ultimate American patriarch, where one expects Whiteness, and more to the point, a certain White heterosexual masculinity at the highest level. It would not be a stretch, then, to suggest that the president implies the "ultimate White man." This, of course, is underscored by the central notion of the White Anglo Saxon Protestant that informs much of America's dominant racial imagery.

Yet, Clinton broke with most of the conventions normally associated with the White masculinity of, say, a Ronald Reagan or a George Bush. While understanding the presidency through the lens of race would seem curious by some, it is important to point out that though there was an obvious generational difference between Clinton, Reagan, and Bush, as was often discussed, with Clinton being routinely described as the first baby boomer president, it is the racial component that proves useful here, and it is this notion of race that best exposes America's cultural movement throughout late-twentieth-century culture.

Stoned Is the Way of the Walk

I'm dreamin' bout a reefer five feet long. Not too fat and not too strong. I wanna get high, but not for long.

—Fats Waller, "You'se a Viper"

Liar, liar/pants on fire/I smoke so much dope/they call me Snoopy Pryor/Which way is up?/I'm tryin' to get higher/I won't stop puffin'/'til I retire.

—Snoop Dogg, "True Lies"

Life's a bitch/and then you die/that's why we get high/cause you never know when you gonna go.

—Nas, "Life's a Bitch"

A good example of Clinton's stylistic difference from previous presidents can be found in the original accusation against his having smoked "weed," though he suggested, now infamously, that he did not inhale. This, too, is informed by an underlying discourse on race in America. If we go back to the origins of marijuana in America, we will find that this has always been an issue with a racial subtext.

It is argued by author Jill Jonnes, in *Hep-Cats, Narcs, and Pipe Dreams: A History of America's Romance with Illegal Drugs,* that the drug marijuana originally made its way into America from the Caribbean through ports like New Orleans, and from there made its way through the Black community into other parts of the country. Much of the early hysteria surrounding weed had to do with the fact that the drug was thought to be the exclusive domain of the jazz world, a world that, of course was, overwhelmingly Black. Thus, when one considers weed paranoia as represented in something like the film *Reefer Madness* (1937), we can now understand this concern to really be about the infiltration of White society by this presumably Black scourge.

One could argue that many drugs in the cultural history of America have had a racial subtext, and the concurrent images, be they of Black crack dealers, Chinese opium dens, or Colombian drug lords, demonstrate this to the fullest. This subtext tends to inform efforts to stop the drugs from moving into mainstream White society. Though in the 1960s weed would become closely associated with the hippie counterculture, this too was an open rejection of what was considered as acceptable as mainstream White behavior during this time.

When one acknowledges the way in which hip hop culture has embraced weed and the culture of weed so strongly, it is again a demonstration of a racially specific notion of the drug and its usage. There have been many hip hop artists who not only speak about smoking but embrace weed as an essential component of any hip hop narrative. Like the great Louis "Pops" Armstrong of old, who smoked virtually every day of his adult life, Dr. Dre—like the Rastafarians before him—on his signature album, *The Chronic* (1992), one of the most important records in the history of music, uses the metaphor of weed as an all-encompassing life force. This is not to suggest that only Black people smoke, no, as Stacy says in The *Wood* (1999), "[N]ame me one race don't smoke weed? Shit, weed is universal!" Yet, it is to suggest that our image of drugs and the drug culture in America is rooted in a racially specific discourse as to its users, sellers, and the often assumed associated social problems.

Even in an otherwise powerful critique of America's failed drug war, like the one forwarded in Steven Soderberg's film *Traffic* (2000), the real evil revolves around a young, upper-class, White girl who is "turned out" on drugs and eventually is seen trading sex for dope with a Black drug dealer in the heart of the ghetto. This image is used to suggest how far she has fallen, and it is also used to suggest the ultimate tragedy of drugs in America, the fact that otherwise innocent White people, here strengthened by the vulnerability of a teenage girl, might be consumed by this larger, uncontrollable Black menace. This is not unlike the lingering suspicions of Black male rape of a White woman, foregrounded in D. W. Griffith's *Birth of a Nation* (1915), and certainly extended by many historical circumstances since that time. So the accusation against Clinton for smoking weed cannot be divorced from this history and it needs to be understood with this racial subtext now firmly on the surface.

Kinda Like Mel Gibson and Danny Glover . . .

One of the most interesting images to emerge during the Clinton presidency was his close friendship with Washington insider and power broker Vernon Jordan. Jordan's name will be forever linked with the Monica Lewinsky scandal, but Jordan's own biography in public life goes back even further.

In 1981, when Jordan was head of the widely recognized civil rights organization the Urban League, he was shot by a potential assassin while jogging with a White female companion in Indiana. Although he may have faded from public life after this, he did not disappear. Making the transition from civil rights leader to political insider, Jordan would eventually go on to become a fixture in Washington power circles and was selected by Clinton to lead his transition team into the White House in 1992. The Urban League, unlike the NAACP, for instance, has always been a civil rights organization more interested in economic empowerment than, say, policy concerns. Thus Jordan's transition was not as much of a change as some might suggest.

To my mind, Vernon Jordan is arguably the most powerful African American in the history of the United States. Considering his behind-the-scenes Michael Corleone–style, his direct influence on the president, and his close connections to the real corridors of power, he is unrivaled as an African American power broker.

Jordan's power, though, would be played out quite differently when we consider how his name emerged during the Lewinsky scandal. It is Jordan's representation as Clinton's close personal friend that is important here.

When asked by a *Newsweek* reporter what he and the president talked about when they were golfing, Jordan replied, "[W]e talk about pussy." Of course, this comment did not do much to help Clinton's eventual scandal, but it did say a great deal about the racial politics of representation.

One of the consistently lingering stereotypes about Black men has to do with a perceived sexual prowess that defines and distinguishes their very existence. Of course, this perception is rooted in the vulgar pathology of slavery and has continued to inform Black male perception since that time. Yet, unlike other negative stereotypes that many people would openly reject, you will seldom find a Black man willing to denounce this particular one. The image of the Black sexual stud, similar to the controversial word "nigga," has now been embraced by Black males, almost unequivocally. Jordan embodies this quite clearly.

His shooting, for instance, can in some way can be read as certain martyrdom. To be shot while jogging with a White woman in a state with a racial history as tattered as Indiana's, conjures up all of those images that worked to prohibit interracial unions, again calling forth *The Birth of a Nation.* From as far back as Shakespeare's *Othello,* to the more recent O.J. Simpson saga—not to mention an uncanny performance of Othello by actor Lawrence Fishburne in a 1995 film version, that seemed to echo what was being played out in court daily during the Simpson trial—suggests to us that the sexually provocative image of a Black male and a White female are embedded in our collective psyche. This theme was revisited and here also linked with the game of basketball and the music of hip hop in Tim Blake Nelson's modern rendering of Othello in his film *O* (2001).

James Toback's film *Black and White* (2000) exemplifies this as well. The film opens with three young Black kids running through Central Park. As they venture deeper and deeper into the more secluded area of the park, they stumble upon a "freak fest," Power, a Black male, and real-life member of the Wu Tang Clan is enjoying himself in the company of two young White women, as they engage in a "threesome." One of Power's bodyguards watches out, with a gun ready to fire on any potential intruders, which he eventually uses when the boys unsuspectingly come onto the scene.

Toback arrives at this scene very deliberately, as if to suggest that behind the facade of normalcy, everyday life, these highly charged sexual acts are taking place. There is something potentially shocking and simultaneously inviting about this scene, for one cannot deny that the overdetermination of the Black male/White female scenario in our culture inevitably works in a seductive and erotic fashion. There is something about the forbidden, and in many ways this can be called the ultimate forbidden in American culture, which tends to fascinate.

Throughout Washington, Vernon Jordan is regarded as a "ladies' man." This was confirmed in a *Sixty Minutes* segment on Jordan during the Lewinsky scandal. Mike Wallace found several prominent White women who commented on Jordan's distinction, his undeniable attraction, and his popularity among the White women in the elite circles that he travels in.

So when Jordan said, in reference to his conversations with Clinton, that "we talk pussy," he was not trying to avoid the well-known accusations against Clinton as a womanizer; instead, in this tradition of what James Brown might call a "sex machine," Jordan was substantiating this reputation. In many ways, one can imagine Clinton's wanting to say this himself, but, of course, this would not work. Yet, his friend, his "homie," if you will, can say it for him, and by virtue of the racial and sexual history of Blackness, the comment can be considered to carry even more weight. Notice, Clinton never denied Jordan's statement.

In many ways, Jordan was commenting on the nature of their friendship, using the sexual as a way of suggesting a familiarity and intimate exclusive knowledge of the president that few other people could claim to have. Jordan, like Snoop Dogg before him, was simply saying, "[I]t ain't no fun, if the homies can't have none."

Jordan's friendship with Clinton parallels the embattled president's embrace by several figures in the hip hop community. One of the primary traditions in hip hop is what is called the "shout out," which is a verbal acknowledgement of a particular person, neighborhood, or city. To receive a shout out in a hip hop song is a one of the highest forms of respect and praise that one could possibly imagine. It is an honor, indeed.

Well, New Orleans rap mogul, Master P dedicates his cut "Dear Mr. President" to "the realest nigga I know, the President." P goes on to suggest that "we want you to know, we feel your pain down here in the ghetto." These statements were made on P's album *Da Last Don* in 1998 after the Republican Party had launched its latest "right wing conspiracy" in the words of Hillary Clinton, against Clinton during the Lewinsky scandal.

To "keep it real" is to shun any notions of pretense, and to remain true to oneself, one's 'hood, and overall to the culture of hip hop. In hip hop, to be considered real is a compliment of the highest order. So maybe even more significant than the act of the shout out itself is the fact that P referred to Clinton as real.

What is it about Clinton, then, that would make him such a viable, even sympathetic figure in the ultramasculine Black world of hip hop? It certainly was not any political agenda geared toward improving the lives of Black people. No. As a matter of fact, Clinton's popularity with African Americans comes almost in spite of the fact that he did very little during his presidency in the way of embracing policy that could be said to favor traditional civil rights concerns. This is what is so amazing about the unrivaled popularity Clinton commanded with African American audiences and especially hip hop audiences who would otherwise be considered uninterested, even hostile to traditional political concerns.

First of all, Clinton's record relative to issues that directly or indirectly would be thought to benefit Black people is really pretty unremarkable. Going back to the election of 1992, Clinton singled out Sista Souljah, a staunchly Black nationalist rapper, for lyrics he characterized as filled with the same hate as the words of the noted right-wing political figure David Duke. Clinton's attack on Sista Souljah was thought by many to be a move that would distance him from powerful civil rights leader Jesse Jackson and send a strong message to the mainstream White constituency that Clinton was not easily manipulated by the civil rights leadership. Sista Souljah's musical career was nonexistent from this point forward.

Not long after the election, Clinton nominee Lani Guinier was effectively "left hangin'" by the president when conservatives attacked her as being too liberal on issues like affirmative action. Though Guinier was said to be a close personal friend of the first family, Clinton simply let her and her nomination die when the heat from the Republicans became too vocal. Guinier, like Sista Souljah, was simply another sacrificial lamb used to bolster Clinton's credentials as a moderate Democrat who was not functioning at the whim of the special interest groups, read, civil rights. Add to this, a similar treatment of the progressive surgeon general Joycelyn Elders, and Clinton's signing of welfare reform legislation that many saw as directly capitulating to conservative racial hostility, and one has a president whose record on matters of race is very unspectacular, even lukewarm, on these highly charged political issues.

This notwithstanding, it should be pointed out that Clinton did begin a dialogue on race and commission a panel led by many prominent Americans of color to initiate public interest in discussing race. He also, and here I think most importantly, did create a climate in which race was treated with a very different degree of seriousness than had any other president in history, by far. The more recent move of his office to Harlem, if for no other reason than the affirmative symbolism it provides, also signifies a strong commitment to embracing people of color in a way unheard of before his presidency.

Clinton enjoys unprecedented popularity among African Americans, and he was perceived as being overly sympathetic to their concerns while in office. One could argue that John F. Kennedy, whose work on civil rights was a lot less engaged than many believe, was also perceived to be a "friend of Black people," in spite of his somewhat ambivalent actions. This is not to suggest that Clinton was ambivalent or openly hostile to Black people either, for again he created a favorable disposition in regard to race that is simply unchallenged by any other president. What this does demonstrate, though, is the power of imagery: Clinton's persona and his personal narrative are such that the combination of the two would override the real policy examples that took place during his tenure in office.

Funky President

Toni Morrison suggests in her prescient October 5, 1998, piece in the *New Yorker*, written at the height of the Lewinsky scandal, that Clinton's appeal has to do with a familiar set of tropes that are most often linked with the long narrative of racial hostility toward African Americans as it has played out in the American imagination and in real-life circumstances, as well. Morrison figuratively places the president into the mix of perceived Blackness when she states, "Clinton displays almost every trope of blackness: single-parent household, born poor, working class, saxophone playing, McDonald's-and-junk food-loving boy from Arkansas" (39).

Many would use these mediated examples to underscore Clinton's differences from previous presidents; others, particularly African Americans, could find a shared experience in his personal narrative because these exaggerated tropes circulate throughout what is often thought to be the "Black experience." Numerous images of Clinton sitting amongst African Americans church congregations would also help to underline this perception.

Yet, the real point of connection had to do with the repeated attacks that Clinton endured during his presidency, and the way he would rebound from each, seemingly stronger than before. African Americans have a long history to draw on when it comes to finding examples of the rug's being pulled out from under a promising career. One of the oldest assumptions about Black success in America is that once one has made it to a point of success and respectability, something devious is done to undermine these gains.

This, of course, goes beyond perception, for there are a multitude of historical examples that would demonstrate this pattern in no uncertain terms. African Americans, in this equation, especially African American men, evidenced by their large numbers in both prison and in the cemetery, are perceived as targets, waiting to be fired upon by those who have no interest in seeing Black societal progress. Similar to the famous Public Enemy logo of a Black man in the crosshairs of a rifle scope, one is thought to be targeted for destruction by a hostile White menace, be it literal or figurative.

Morrison goes on to say,

> No matter how smart you are, how hard you work, how much coin you earn for us, we will put you in your place, or put you out of the place you have somehow, albeit with our permission, achieved. You will be fired from your job, sent away in disgrace, and—who knows?—maybe sentenced and jailed to boot. In short, unless you do as we say (i.e., assimilate at once), your expletives belong to us.

These comments certainly sum up the thoughts of many African Americans who have had more than enough experience with circumstances such as the ones implied by Morrison's illuminating prose. This is not to suggest that African American women do not experience their own forms of racial discrimination, yet it is important to point out that gender differences would suggest racism's operating somewhat differently in this regard.

When one considers that being born a Black male in American society is an immediate strike against one, as the high prison and cemetery populations imply, and that as one goes through life many actual events confirm this sense, one finds that Clinton's constant battles, often over his private life, fit neatly into this larger Black scenario.

The viciousness of Clinton's attackers here again invokes the *playa hater*. Oftentimes in hip hop, the haters come from the same camp as the person being hated on. This notion of the playa hater is an apt description of the way that many of Clinton's opponents were like him and of his generation. Deposed Speaker of the House and playa hater par excellence Newt Gingrich, also a southerner and of Clinton's generation, provides a perfect example here. Mississippi senator Trent Lott and Georgia representative Bob Barr serve as good examples of the hate scenario also.

One could argue, for instance, that the attacks on Clinton were really an extension of the ideological battles being fought in the late 1960s around civil rights, Vietnam, women's rights, and so on. Though one might suspect that this era had passed, the liberal/conservative differences of that time had come to the surface again, now that the baby boom generation had come to power. This time though, they were fighting it out in the corridors of power, as opposed to the way things were done in their youthful college days.

Remember, for instance, the way that the media would compare Clinton's path in life to that of his most visible hater, special prosecutor Ken Starr. Though both men were of the same generation, the two went separate ideological ways. When one considers that after several attempts, long investigations, and large amounts of money being spent to bust Clinton on Whitewater and other relative nonissues, the only real charge that could be leveled involved a dubious sexual encounter, the hater in Ken Starr becomes even more obvious.

This was not unlike the government's sting operation on former Washington, D.C., mayor Marion Berry, in which large sums of money were spent over long periods of time to ultimately provide a video of Barry smoking crack with a prostitute. Affairs with interns and crack parties with prostitutes are not necessarily the image most people want to have of their political leaders, but the zealous ideological pursuit of these men by their detractors seems perfectly in line with the notion of the playa hater in hip hop.

Morrison's words, her description of Clinton's predicament, echo many similar narratives throughout hip hop culture. Take, for instance, Jay-Z, the hip hop artist who has made the most of the genre's sense of autobiography. Jay-Z, across his body of work, has emphasized the epic and often cinematic nature of his own life as the vehicle that propels his existence, as well as his music. His albums feature a range of titles that embrace hip hop as the means for articulating one's own life relative to the demands of a hostile society. Titled and subtitled, these albums include, for example, *In My Lifetime, The Hard Knock Life,* and *The Life and Times of*

S. Carter, which, by the way, is a reference to Jay-Z's real name, Shawn Carter. In a genre where most artists use a character name, other than their own, Jay-Z's use of Shawn Carter here stands out. By invoking his own name, he is underscoring the aesthetic of realism that so informs hip hop production.

With each of his records presented as its own volume, the work of Jay-Z can be said to function in the tradition of *The Autobiography of Malcolm X,* Alex Haley's canonical text of urban Black masculinity, as well as one of the canonical texts of late-twentieth-century America. Notice, for instance, Jay-Z's lyrics on the cut "Dope Man" from his 2000 album *The Life and Times of S. Carter* and the way in which these sentiments can be linked to what Morrison suggested about Bill Clinton, the specific nature of Black ghetto existence and southern White working-class existence, notwithstanding.

Set up as though he were in a courtroom speaking to a judge on his own behalf, Jay-Z declares:

> I'm a prisoner of circumstance/Frail nigga/I couldn't much work with my hands/But my mind was strong/I grew where you hold your Blacks up/Trap us, expect us not to pick gats up/Where you drop your crack off by the Mack trucks/Destroy our dreams of lawyers and actors/Keep us spiralin'/goin' backwards/At age nine, saw my first hate crime/Blindfolded/expected to walk a straight line/Mind molded/taught to love you and hate mine/Climbed over it/at a early age/Jay shine/Fuck the system/at Lady Justice I blaze nine/Your Honor/I no longer kill my people/I raise mine/The soul of Mumia in this modern day time.

The inevitability of one's destiny is here defined against the backdrop of a racist America, which has consistently and systematically denied an opportunity for advancement at every turn. The vivid description of a life filled with disappointment and desperation is concluded, though, by a triumphant victory over all obstacles. It is the individual's determination in the face of all odds that makes Jay-Z's stand so empowering. In spite of all the racism placed in front of him, he manages to survive and even uses the journey as a way to embrace a larger social consciousness. This is implied, of course, by the invocation of Mumia Abul-Jamal, the Pennsylvania death row inmate whose writings have made him the most visible martyr of an unjust legal system during the reign of hip hop.

When one accepts the reality of dire circumstances and uses these circumstances as a way to overcome difficulty, instead of perpetrating the negativity, this is success. One is reminded of the classic hip hop group Grand Master Flash and the Furious Five, who long ago talked about "survival, only the strong survive." If nothing else, hip hop is indeed about survival. When in spite of everything they have thrown in the way, one still survives, and not only that but survives and is stronger than before, it is a victory of the highest order.

Clinton's arc functions similarly. A man who once dubbed himself the "comeback kid," who was on the verge of being dismissed after one term, rebounded tremendously after all this, along with weathering the numerous attacks from several powerful playa haters. He went on to overwhelming approval ratings, even higher than those of the beloved patriarch Ronald Reagan. In other words, in spite of it all, Clinton went out on top.

As indicated by the "pimp stroll" he displayed as he walked out through that long corridor at the Staples Center to the applause of the Democratic Convention in 2000, this will forever be his legacy of triumph. One cannot deny the way in which this legacy developed and was nurtured during a time when hip hop provided the words and life lessons with which to understand the overall process.

The Rebirth of the Cool and the Reemergence of the White Negro

During the summer of 1998, while on the set of my debut as a writer, producer, and actor, in *The Wood*, I got into a long conversation about one of that summer's hottest movies, Steven Soderberg's *Out of Sight*.

I eventually decided that I needed to comment on this publicly, and began writing a piece called "A Nod to Cool or a New Blaxploitation" for the *Los Angeles Times* that would detail what I saw as the return of a very prominent figure to the American cultural landscape, that being the fabled "white negro" that Norman Mailer had written so emphatically about back in the late 1950s.

> I've never seen no white pimp, ya know. Mostly everybody that I've seen that's fuckin' wit this is something like myself; Black man. I don't think them other races have the charisma, you know what I mean, to move and shake like a pimp shake.
>
> —Bradley, in The Hughes Brothers' *American Pimp* (2000)

In my mind, George Clooney is only one in a long line of prominent White male actors who had adopted a distinct cultural style so readily associated with Black masculinity. During that same year of 1998, Warren Beatty had generated a great deal of conversation with his film *Bulworth*, in which a cynical disillusioned senator dives headfirst into the world of hip hop culture and emerges to speak an undisputed truth that is now eagerly embraced by a wide swath of voters.

Jack Nicholson, who received an Oscar in 1998 for his work in the film *As Good As It Gets* (1997), began his acceptance speech that year a "shout out," by thanking the person who originally birthed the cool, Miles Davis, as one of his primary inspirations. John Travolta and Bruce Willis, two of the most popular movie stars of their time, could also be included in this group of emergent White negroes.

What I am referring to here as cool, is the persona so often associated with Black men, and the antithesis of what would be described as White masculinity. Cool is about a detached, removed, nonchalant sense of being. An aloofness that suggests one is above it all. A pride, an arrogance even, that is at once laid back, unconcerned, perceived to be highly sexual and potentially violent.

Certainly from the time that young Black men began defining urban space in the 1920s, this often unspoken way of being has distinguished them from the more upright, stiff, and mechanical disposition associated with White men. Lewis MacAdams, for instance, historicizes this notion of the cool phenomenon in his book *Birth of the Cool*, recognizing be bop to be the starting point as it pertains to this expression in culture.

As embodied in the title of something like *White Men Can't Jump* there is a strong sense of physicality and sexuality that informs society's definition of Black masculinity. To the extent that the ultimate expression of the physical, sports, is increasingly defined by Black men in our society, this reaffirms the prevailing sentiment. There is a notion of cool, that is like an utter calm in the eye of a storm, embodied in the metaphor of ice water running through one's veins that tends to inform most of our understanding about Blackness as it functions in America.

In a film like *Out of Sight*, for instance, Clooney is laid back and reserved in his being, and his sense of masculinity is bolstered by the fact that he holds his own in a world otherwise dominated by Black men. For instance, in a congested space that is defined by a strong sense of Black and Brown ultramasculinity, prison, Clooney "runs things," as it were, and is able to demand the loyalty of Ving Rhames and the other hardened Black criminals who make up his crew. Here proximity confers status.

This is not unlike Christopher Walken's character, Frank White, from Abel Ferrer's underground classic *The King of New York* (1990). Frank White, a drug kingpin when released from prison, reassembles his all-Black crew, both male and female, and oscillates in Robin Hood–like fashion, moving between the life of crime and charitable benevolence, all the while planning to build a much-needed hospital in an impoverished neighborhood.

Despite a presumed animosity between Black and White men, especially as it has functioned in Hollywood, and most especially as it has often pitted racial factions against one another when the narrative involves the underworld life, Frank White is cool with all the Brothas, this while mackin' to all the sistas. In other words, he is friends with all the Black men, their homie even, while being the sexual object of choice for the fine Black women who surround him.

Frank White is so cool that the Notorious B.I.G. often referred to himself as the "Black Frank White," for B.I.G. was, without a doubt, the king of New York in his own right. Yet the fact that a distinct icon of contemporary Blackness, Biggie, would appropriate his name from a White character, who had, of course, appropriated his whole being from Black masculinity, is like African American musicians who embrace and redefine rock and roll as Black, when this was the case in the first place. I guess turnabout is fair play?

Clooney in *Out of Sight*, is also able to attract the attention of the film's female lead, Jennifer Lopez, who herself offers a interesting take on the questions of race, gender, and popular culture. What is interesting in the case of Lopez, is that the film chooses to construct her character in such a way so as to downplay race as an issue. While her racially specific appearance is never subtle, the film foregrounds a character who is devoid of surroundings that would suggest race. Yet, one cannot help but think race when looking at her.

As writer Erin Aubrey stated in an article from *Salon* around the release of the film:

> The problem with "Out of Sight" is that Lopez is granted a butt, but it is undone by the fact that her character is so ethnically neutral. The industry is so busy congratulating itself for mainstreaming a possibly African-descended Latina, for putting a body type up front that is not Gwyneth Paltrow flat, that it fails to allow Lopez anything else of interest. Many people will argue that this movie is at least a triumph of multiculturalism—a term that denotes little more than a fuzzy, New Age racism parading around in the sheep's clothing of progress. Divorced from its native attitude, this butt lacks bite.

Aubrey makes some compelling points. It is as though Lopez represents Hollywood's having its racial cake and eating it too. When you consider that Lopez first became visible as a "Fly Girl," a dancer on *In Livin' Color* in the early '90s, and then parlayed this into a starring turn as *Selena*, in the biopic about the late Latina singer who was poised for American superstardom before being tragically murdered, it is difficult not to visualize race as an important cultural marker for her stardom.

Yet, as Lopez would become a more popular, read mainstream, star, much would be done to at least lessen her direct association with race. To the extent that the Black/White racial dichotomy, which is rooted in the slave economy and would go on to define America's cultural identity for years to come, informs much of what goes on in American life, contemporary culture has seen a challenge to this once binary notion of race. With an increasing Latino, Asian, and South Asian dynamic unfolding in America, one finds that the Black/White split is a bit too limiting to fully understand the racial and cultural currents that will undoubtedly define this century.

Lopez is Puerto Rican and from New York. This ethnicity has of course long been a primary fixture in the cultural identity of New York City. In this regard, it has also been closely aligned, in this lived environment, with that of African Americans, as codified in a name like that of "Spanish Harlem," for instance, where language is used to modify a location almost exclusively associated with Blackness in terms of public perception. This, of course, is highlighted in hip hop by the undoubted presence of Puerto Ricans, from the very beginning of hip hop, back in the mid 1970s.

Consider the stature of someone like Fat Joe, or the reverence afforded Big Pun, in his death, this alongside the amazing performance of Benjamin Bratt as one of the creators of Nuyorican poetry, Miguel Pinero, in the film *Pinero* (2001), or the common colloquial use of Spanish words like "Mami" and "Popi" by numerous rappers, including Biggie and Jay-Z, and it is clear that the specific cultural makeup of New York is such that African Americans and Puerto Ricans often occupy the same space and share a similar culture. With this in mind, I find it a bit superficial that some would try to create a racial controversy over J. Lo's use of the word "nigga" in a remix of one of her songs.

Lopez tends to function as *Black* for many who are knowledgeable about these cultural traditions. Her racially distinct ass, and challenge to a dominant standard of beauty, as pointed out in the Aubrey quote, her gig as Fly Girl, her music, and her close connection to the ghetto-fabulous Puffy Combs can be said to further this connection. So, regardless of what the film may do to lessen her race, she is a "nigga," in the most endearing sense of that word, and these visual cues and cultural references remain in place.

Therefore, when Clooney captures her interest in the film, when he succeeds in breaking down her resistance, when he, in effect, puts his own mack game down, he substantiates his role as a White negro who can not only coexist with the Black men in the film but also have the current paragon of Latina/Black femininity without having to give up anything in the process. Like Frank White, Clooney has managed to appropriate Blackness without getting his hands dirty.

> What you think these white people really want from us? You know what I'm talkin' bout? White muthafuckas out here, tryin' to imitate us, tryin' to rap, tryin' to dress Black and all this shit. Bitches throwin' pussy all over . . . what's goin' on wit this shit? Lotta people just think it's like size, you know, the myth; niggas got bigger dicks and shit. But I don't think that's it tho. I think they think they gonna get some kinda life force or some shit from fuckin' wit us.
>
> —Rich Bowers, *Black and White*

So what is at stake here in this discussion of appropriation is the question of power. White culture appropriating from Black culture, White people appropriating from Black people. The appropriation of style is often where the biggest debates take place because nuances of style are intangible. In a world where the authentic is consistently problematized, it is often hard to distinguish where this appropriation takes place.

It is very obvious that Fred Astaire "bit" Bill "Bojangles" Robinson's dance style in a segregated world. Yet the dominant discourse of the time was such that mainstream America was not aware of this appropriation, for Astaire's style was normalized as the benchmark for dance. On the other hand, Black audiences were acutely aware of this but did not have the power to voice any objection. Yet, in a world where at least the cultural landscape is often highly integrated, where hip hop has become a staple on MTV, the cultural benchmark of the late twentieth century and early twenty-first century, these normally subtle appropriations are far from subtle. The appropriations are, like the culture, in your face.

At one point in *Black and White*, Brooke Shields's character, who is a documentary filmmaker working on a film about rich White kids who love the hip hop lifestyle, asks, "Why are you guys always imitating a Black culture, a Black lifestyle?" To which the response is, "We're not imitating it, we're influenced by it." This is a profound statement, and one that needs examining. What is the difference between imitation and influence?

To assume that a culture is being imitated in some way implies a mockery, a cheap alternative to the real thing. It also implies an ownership of something that is being taken from its original proprietors. For a White person to imitate Black culture is seen as being something that the White person is not. Though imitation is considered the sincerest flattery, it is something that in the hip hop era is uniquely frowned upon.

To "bite" someone's style is one of the worst crimes in hip hop. In a genre of music so tied to individual expression, any overt imitation of someone else's style is considered the ultimate act of inauthentic existence. You are considered a fake, a *fugazzi*, a pale imitation of the original. In a world where to "keep it real" defines the mood, "jockin" someone's style is about as far from the real as one can be.

In one of the first instances of the intrusion of Whiteness in hip hop, a sub-urban White kid from Dallas, Rob Van Winkel, better known as Vanilla Ice, was thought to be an imitator of the highest order. He fabricated a story about a trou-bled ghetto upbringing, he bit a popular Black fraternity slogan, and was even charged, by the notorious Death Row Records head, Suge Knight, with stealing writing credit for his popular song "Ice, Ice, Baby," from a Black collaborator.

Though Ice sold a ton of records, he was immediately dismissed in hip hop circles as a fraud, a feeble attempt to cash in on hip hop's burgeoning success with an Elvislike move of exploitation. Ice was off the scene before really getting on it. He has become a footnote to an earlier time in hip hop, a cruel joke played on the public, masquerading in the guise of reality. Even mainstream White America saw through the cheap toilet-paper-thin presence of such a bad actor. This is imitation.

On the other hand, to say that you are influenced by something tends to function somewhat differently. To admit influence is to immediately give credit where it is due, to acknowledge the source of something taken. In the parlance of hip hop, it is the equivalent of giving "props," which is considered of high impor-tance.

Hip hop has always placed a great worth on making connections to a larger historical sense of the culture, thus the lofty status accorded to the idea of an "old school." In this regard, one is expected to recognize one's origins, and always main-tain a strong connection to this history. Not only in terms of one's own life and family but also in terms of the music itself. The shout out is a call of recognition for your homies, your family, your neighborhood, your crew. It can also be an ac-knowledgment of those figures considered estimable within the genre itself or other artists, athletes, or political figures from earlier eras who are deemed appro-priate for hip hop culture. This respect is evident, for instance, in all the tributes that have been made to fallen hip hop icons like Tupac and Biggie.

As each new generation of hip hop artists emerges, they continue this sense of legacy. Snoop can admit the influence that Slick Rick and Too Short had on him, and then Biggie and Jay-Z can in turn foreground Snoop's influence on their work. This is considered an act of respect that still allows the artist to maintain his or her sense of individuality. Jay-Z, for instance, often takes snippets of other people's famous lines and places them in the service of his own lyrics. This is similar to the way that an artist like Robert Rauschenberg might use the idea of collage, or like Andy Warhol might take a popular everyday image and make it his own unique rendition.

In the summer of 1998, the hip hop collective Ruff Ryders, known for their signature artist DMX and the Casio-keyboard-enhanced sound of their main producer, Swizz Beats, released a compilation of songs featuring their beats, with lyrics provided by a host of other prominent rappers.

The best cut on the record was a track by Jay-Z called "Jigga, My Nigga," which begins with the lines "Sold crack when I was down in AC/back on the block/Jay-Z muthafucka from the, the, the Roc/went solo on that ass but it's still the same/Brooklyn be the place where I serve them thangs." This line is directly lifted from Snoop's famous 1993 single "Who Am I (What's My Name?)." Snoop says, "From the depths of the sea/back to the block/Snoop Doggy Dogg/funky/yes but of the Doc/went solo on that ass/but it's still the same/Long Beach is the spot where I served my caine."

The Snoop reference is too obvious to miss. "Who Am I?" was the first single from Snoop's long-awaited solo album *Doggystyle* (1993). After redefining hip hop in 1992 with the release of Dr Dre's *The Chronic*, Snoop's voice would become one of the most highly regarded in hip hop. Yet, until the release of *Doggystyle*, Snoop was still seen only as a great player on Dre's team. This album would be the first to exclusively foreground Snoop as a star in his own right, and "Who Am I?" was the bold declaration of this new identity. Not only does he mention that he is now a solo act, he also points to his celebrated home of Long Beach.

Dr. Dre and Snoop had become the most visible faces in hip hop and they personified what was now being referred to as a unique West Coast style, which of course, was very distinct from what had traditionally come out of New York. So not only was "Who Am I?" about identity, it was also about location. In the ensuing East Coast/West Coast conflict that engulfed hip hop for a few years in the mid '90s, Snoop was considered a symbol emblematic of the West Coast. In the video for Tha Dogg Pound's "New York, New York," a few years later when the bicoastal rivalry was in full effect, Snoop is pictured, larger than life, marching through New York City, crushing several high-rise buildings underfoot, as he symbolically walks all over the East Coast.

Jay-Z, on the other hand, is most closely associated with his friend and fellow Brooklynite, the late Biggie Smalls. This is decidedly East Coast. So for an East Coast rapper to "bite" West Coast, period, this would be thought questionable by some, even in the aftermath of the rivalry itself. To "bite" Snoop, whose utter act of disrespect was also greeted with gunfire during the video shoot, would force even more to question this particular style choice, for Snoop is eminently symbolic of the West Coast. Yet, Jay-Z, using similar cadence, acknowledges Snoop, for the line is too well known not to recognize it immediately, yet he changes it up, and specifies it to Brooklyn. He has admitted Snoop's influence and at the same time made his own personal statement.

Thus, influence says that one is open to be inspired by something potentially outside one's own environment. In regard to the character's statement in *Black and White,* then, the fact that these rich White kids are influenced by Black culture, suggests that they are open to it, and it also suggests the power of Black culture to infiltrate the masses, a charge that has not always been acknowledged or welcomed. It suggests that Black culture has the power to influence and that this influence is transcendent. The recognition and articulation of this power is something that has only recently been uttered by elements of White society. This is a good example of agency, which allows us to think of Black culture in much more complex ways, not simply as something being plundered and victimized by potential exploiters but as a vibrant, energetic, and empowered social and cultural force that can potentially influence anyone with whom it comes in contact, as it has done for all these years anyway.

Play That Funky Music, White Boy

> The strangest things can happen/in rappin'/when/niggas get wrapped up in image and acting.
>
> —Dr. Dre (cowritten with Eminem), "The Watcher"

If one were to foreground influence as it functions in hip hop, then, a discussion of the influence of this otherwise Black form on White performers seems to begin and end with Eminem. Hailing from a working-class suburb of Detroit, Em, like his fellow suburban Detroit homies, Kid Rock, Elmore Leonard, and even Madonna, were directly confronted with Black culture in ways specific to the nature of Black Detroit. In a city where Black and White tend to be severely divided along stark geographical lines, the dominant culture is defiantly one that favors Black culture, almost unequivocally. Because of a majority Black population, with much political power, and a long history of defiant Black nationalist thought embedded in the discourse of the city, Blackness is everywhere and in force. It is most evident in cultural expression. There are, of course, White people who hate this, and then there are those who find it to be the most empowering force in their sense of cultural identity.

I am reminded of a White college friend of Polish ethnicity from Detroit who often said that until he was in third grade, when his family was finally able to afford the move to the 'burbs, that he thought that White people were a minority in this country, based on the overwhelming Blackness that surrounded him in his Detroit neighborhood. The many conversations that I have had with my homie, David Was, he of the band Was Not Was, and the influence the city had on his cultural makeup in the formative years also inform my thoughts on this issue.

Thus, Em, like the other figures I have named, was in a position where he could easily be influenced by the culture because it was present in his environment. Add to this, Em's "poor White trash" influences and you have the makings of Slim Shady. Mind you, he is not a White boy who wants to be Black, he is *Black*, yet his appearance simply happens to be White. This is still America, and yes, skin color still matters, in most, if not all things. Even so, to the extent that hip hop has defined the real as rooted in a marginal, poverty-stricken, pathologically defined existence, then Em is potentially more *Black than* many of the middle-class and wealthy Black people who live in mainstream White society today. In other words, to me, Em is a nigga. No doubt.

We cannot question his authenticity, nor can we question his right to rap, considering that hip hop culture has been out in the open and ready to be appropriated for so long. There are now legions of White youths in America who have never even listened to any other kind of music. Em is a hip hop head, a B boy, of the highest order. His intimate familiarity with the culture comes through loud and clear in his raps.

That being said, he is worthy of discussion for his presence on the hip hop scene, with the least important aspect of this discussion being his controversial lyrics. Eminem the rapper is okay, better than some, not as good as others. Eminem the White nigga, though, is something that requires much more attention.

In the time since the release of *The Slim Shady LP* in 1999, the rapper also known as Eminem has captured the attention of the American public. Music critics nationwide have celebrated and critiqued his work like the treatment reserved for only those truly considered giants in the music industry. Em's appearance with Elton John at the 2001 Grammy ceremony has to be one of the most overpublicized stunts since Geraldo Rivera went strolling through Al Capone's vault. In an era when the derivative blandness of the so-called boy and girl groups dominated record sales, music writers were hungry like the werewolf of London

to find something of interest to talk about and Slim Shady proved to be the ben-
eficiary.

What is most troubling is that Eminem is taken seriously, this in a world
where the genre of music he works in, hip hop, has routinely been ignored at best
and rejected at worst. Though there has been much written about hip hop, it has
often been writing of a dismissive nature.

Yet, with Eminem, the writers went about engaging not only the artist but his
lyrics and his music as well. Even in the harsh critiques of Eminem's music by
many writers, because of his often overt nihilistic, sexist, and homophobic remarks, there is still a sense of respect for the artist and his music, with a constant
analysis of the fundamental freedom of speech inherent in these reviews. This
posits Em as someone and something to talk about, debate, and in turn, be treated
as a serious cultural subject, a seriousness that has often eluded discussions of hip
hop as it pertains to Black artists.

This discourse is not unlike that which accompanied the arrival and presence
of basketball's Larry Bird in the 1980s. As I have argued elsewhere, Bird was a player
whose ability to play the game of basketball at a high level is unquestioned. He is
certainly one of the best players ever to have played the game, and his historical
significance is central in understanding the transition of the National Basketball
Association from a marginal league into a league that often received enormous
media coverage around the globe. Yet, during his playing days, he often functioned
as a latter-day "great White hope" for many of the sports writers and broadcasters
who control the discourse around the game of basketball.

Bird's style of play, for instance, was such that he seldom relied on overly
physical moves but, instead, used a nearly perfect fundamental interpretation and
execution of the game to his benefit. This style was often contrasted against a
more physical style of play that is often associated with Black players, and thus
Bird was thought to be defying his limitations, his lack of assumed physical gifts,

and succeeding in a league where it was the accepted wisdom that White men could not jump.

What was always interesting about this argument was that Bird's most visible opponent during these days, Magic Johnson, had a similar style of play, yet this was almost completely ignored by those who control the rhetoric of sport. Even though Magic was very tall for the position he played, point guard, he was not known for his excessive physical skills. He was not known for his gravity-defying dunks or other such moves that would normally be inherent in a playground style; his signature "no look" pass, might be a minor exception here. No, Magic was known for his court vision, his basketball intelligence, his consistently winning ways, and ultimately, his unrivaled abilities as the leader of his team. In other words, Magic Johnson, a Black man, had what many would call a "White man's game." Yet, during his playing days, Magic was seldom regarded in this way, and Bird was spoken and thought of in this way exclusively.

Magic and Bird's style would be in direct contrast to that of Michael Jordan, who tended to dominate games from a physical standpoint, especially early in his career, before he resorted to an intellectual and psychological dominance in the latter years. Often though, he would dominate from all three of these areas at once.

It is Michael's legacy as a dunker that earned much of his early reputation. Having won the NBA's dunk contest as a rookie, Jordan would go on to win a dramatic and now legendary dunk contest with Dominique Wilkins in 1988, and this is what contributed most to his image, prior to winning championships in the 1990s.

Jason Williams, now of the Memphis Grizzlies, offers another example. Jay Dub began receiving a great deal of attention for his over-the-top style on the basketball court during the shortened 1999 NBA season as a member of the Sacramento Kings. Once Williams started appearing in the nightly highlight shows, there was an immediate movement afoot to find a suitable nickname for this emerging

White player. Though "White chocolate" became the most popular, all of the nicknames had Blackness. When trying to find an appropriate player to whom to compare Williams, the league, as well as the sports media, began comparing him to "Pistol" Pete Maravich, a White player from the 1970s.

The fact that Williams played with a style that is closely associated with the playground, and by extension, Blackness, he was said to have some "Black" in his game. Yet no one would take the next step and compare him directly to a Black player. As a matter of fact, Williams is too young to have seen Maravich play, and though he is now certainly knowledgeable about Maravich at this point, it is more likely that Williams's style emerged from watching more contemporary Black players such as Isiah Thomas, Magic Johnson, and even Allen Iverson.

Second, the style that Williams plays has always been critiqued by the sports establishment as too selfish and too flashy, and overall, it has been discouraged when performed by Black players. Yet when Williams uses this playground style it becomes acceptable, and suitable to be promoted? Considering that Williams's jersey was at one time the best-selling jersey in the league, we can clearly see the continued longing for another "great White hope."

Embedded here was a perception of Black physical superiority, and thus, any White player who overcame these assumed limitations, these racially specific disadvantages was thought to be deserving of much praise. Overall, it was thought that Black players started out with an advantage and thus their overwhelming success in the game should be assumed, and therefore, commonplace, run of the mill, and ultimately of less significance than that of a White player who has had to overcome a multitude of physical and, to some extent, cultural limitations.

It is interesting how the reversal of this argument has never worked for Black people in America, as the clear and obvious disadvantages of slavery are often dismissed as having no real impact on today's society and thus measures to "balance the playing field," as it were, like affirmative action, are deemed to place White people at an even stronger disadvantage.

Once, in early 2001, while participating on a panel sponsored by the Anti-Defamation League, the moderator, *Spin* magazine editor Alan Light, posed a question about Eminem, a topic that was being widely discussed in public at that time because of the enormous attention Em's multiple Grammy nominations had garnered. Having felt that the public was making too much fuss about Em, having ignored or dismissed hip hop prior to this point, I simply did not want to add to this overblown attention that the rapper was receiving. Knowing that the question would come up, though, I felt it also a bit predictable.

Why was hip hop so important now? Was it simply because the central figure being discussed was a White boy? With these thoughts informing my words, I jokingly said, as I often do, "Fuck Eminem!" Yet, as they say, a lot of truth is spoken in jest. My response was also intended to highlight the way in which Whiteness had begun to obfuscate another Black cultural form. Why were we talking about Em, when we had never spent this much time seriously talking about say the poetic lyrics of Rakim, Lil' Kim's nuanced gender critique, Talib Kweli's political soul, or Biggie's vivid Scorcesesque cinematic descriptions of the life?

One might suspect that my words generated a vocal response, and this is true, they did. The response, though, was not from the audience members, who were truly digging what I was saying, no the response was from another panelist, who was supposed to be there representing hip hop.

Neb Luv is a young female rapper, formerly of The Five Footers. The group is featured in the hip hop documentary *The Show* (1995), in a humorously petty situation where their producer, Warren G, is arguing that the Five Footers do not need to pay a hairdresser while on the road because their hair is braided.

Neb Luv vocally disagreed with my comments, and interrupted my flow to say that, in essence, we must realize how hard it was for Em to make it as a White rapper, we must be sympathetic to his struggles, and respect the fact that he had overcome many cultural obstacles on the way to superstardom.

This ridiculous statement reminded me of the comments of Mr. Whitefolks, a White pimp, featured in the HBO documentary *Pimps Up, Hoes Down* (1998). Mr. Whitefolks says that early on in his decision to become a pimp, he faced discrimination based on his race from the Black pimps. Yet, he proudly says that when they saw how good he was at the game that they quickly began to recognize his skills and show him the respect he deserves for being a true cross-country pimp.

Imagine, in a world where racism is still rampant and now deeply embedded in the collective psyche of America, where Black and Brown men populate the penitentiary and the graveyard in record numbers, where "driving while Black or Brown" is considered a crime by many law enforcement officers, amongst other things, that we would be discussing how hard it was for a White boy to make it as a pimp or a rap artist. This is absurd. About as absurd as the *Sports Illustrated* cover of December 8, 1997, that asked, with a straight face, "What Ever Happened to the White Athlete?"

The comments of Neb Luv, though, point to something deeper. Her desire to celebrate Eminem is a position held by many other Black rappers. It is almost as though these rappers bend over backward to praise Em's skills and in turn *accept* him as a member of the hip hop community. This expression of what I have called "Black guilt" operates similarly to what has often been described as liberal White guilt.

The assumption goes that certain liberal White people feel guilty about racism and thus often allow this guilt to cloud their dealings with Black people. And it is assumed that this feeling motivates them to overcompensate, to go out of their way to prove their liberalism. The power dynamic not withstanding, Black guilt functions in the same way.

Though this is often unspoken, many Black people feel that if a White person simply shows some attention, indicates some affection for the culture, that this is reason for gratitude. When Isiah Thomas stated that Larry Bird was overrated because of his race, several Black players around the league jumped to Bird's defense, in the same way that many of Black rappers have jumped to Em's defense.

There is at some level a sense of inferiority, potentially a bit of self-hatred, and an acceptance that anything deemed Black in this society is somehow of lesser value than something defined as White. When a White person like Em decides to enter this arena, it is as though his Whiteness raises the profile of the culture in question. The culture is now considered significant because a White person finds it worth his or her time to participate in this Black cultural form. It is as though the White person is doing the culture a favor of sorts.

In addition, the presence of Whiteness brings certain legitimacy to the form and the response is a resounding thank you, which can here be expressed through the way in which Neb Luv and others come rushing to Eminem's defense. What I am getting at is that the presence of Whiteness is often thought to make something more serious, more legitimate, and this exposes a cultural inferiority complex on the part of many Black artists and audiences

One is reminded of Malcolm X's metaphoric dichotomy of the house nigga and the field nigga. In this equation the house nigga "tries harder than the master" to put out a fire that is consuming the master's house. The house nigga has bought so deeply into the master's program that the master's best interests become the slave's best interests as well. So many African Americans have bought into the perceptions of dominant society regarding their own existence, that even in a potentially resistant form like hip hop, they see it necessary to defend what in another time might have been thought to be an attempt at exploitation.

It is not unlike Bill Clinton moving his office to Harlem, another act of attention that suggests that Harlem has now come up, considering that the White man has moved in. When one ponders the redevelopment efforts that have taken place in Harlem more recently, the arrival of Starbucks and the Gap, for instance, they again work to raise Harlem's image by virtue of a White presence.

It was not as though Harlem was Clinton's first choice, far from it. Instead, Harlem becomes a way to respond to his critics, especially those who questioned the expenses of the office space he originally coveted in midtown. Knowing that he would receive a resounding welcome in Harlem, Clinton here uses location as a way of communicating his animosity toward his playa hatin' enemies.

The use of Harlem is not unlike Eminem's use of hip hop. Em clothes himself in the Blackness of hip hop, and then points his two middle fingers upward as a statement to his more mainstream detractors. Blackness here is a sign of defiance, particularly when embraced by a White male, who compounds his attempts at otherness when merging Blackness with a "poor White trash" disposition. To the extent that hip hop represents a defiant sense of urban Black masculinity, Eminem can benefit from this and use it against his detractors, while being defended by other Black figures in the genre, his bodyguards if you will, and without having to do any of the work that goes along with it, namely, growing up poor and Black in America.

Clinton is no different, when you consider that his default move to Harlem shields him from the haters who now have an entire community to get through before getting at the former president. Blackness becomes the shield from White criticism and the Black space, be it Harlem or hip hop, is considered enhanced by the presence of the proverbial White man. In the same way that Vernon Jordan assisted in foregrounding Clinton's sexual prowess, here the location of Harlem underscores his defiant rejection of White space. With all this taking place though, it is important to point out that neither Clinton nor Eminem has to stop being White in order to enjoy these privileges. Blackness is then seen as a cloak of defiance, which can be discarded at any moment, when this cloak is no longer fashionable.

Eminem though, like Clinton, also needed an entry pass, a sponsor of sorts. For Clinton, of course, it was Vernon Jordan, and for Eminem, it was Dr. Dre. This is where we know times have changed. What ultimately distinguishes Eminem from Elvis here is that the racism of the times made it such that he need not consult Black culture before going in to plunder it. No, Elvis, Colonel Tom Parker, and Sam Phillips simply housed all the Black shit they could and went on to fame, fortune, and superstardom, without ever being concerned with what the people whose music they were stealing might have to say about the matter. This is no longer possible. As demonstrated by the hostile rejection of an earlier White imposter, Vanilla Ice, hip hop has been long poised to dismiss any potential perpetrator in a genre of music rooted in a quest for authenticity. The rumors of Suge Knight's holding Ice outside a hotel window to gain control of the publishing credit that Ice stole from a Black rapper substantiates this fact in a most obvious way.

Eminem, of course has never faced this type of rejection. Quite the contrary. He has been, as I have mentioned already, overwhelmingly embraced. A great deal of this has to do with the fact that he was introduced to the hip hop audience by a true hip hop luminary, Dr. Dre. This endorsement cannot be underestimated.

Hip hop has always been a movement interested in history, particularly its own. When considering that many rappers come and go with increased regularity, be it from poor record sales, incarceration, or in some cases, death, Dr. Dre's long tenure in the game makes him stand out. Not only has he been around for quite some time, he has been instrumental in advancing the artistry of hip hop through his unrivaled skills as a producer. As one of the founding members of the highly significant group NWA, Dre went on to redefine hip hop with the release of *The Chronic* in 1992, and a string of hit albums that would follow on the notorious Death Row record label.

Dre reinterpreted '70s soul, especially funk master George Clinton, and in doing so, he went on to create something that will forever stand out in hip hop. *The Chronic* is an album that exemplifies an extremely sophisticated production and one that also represents an expression of the most entrenched street sensibilities. For these reasons, he can endorse Em and provide for him the cultural credibility that would not necessarily be available to Em on his own.

Hip hop redefines the circumstances of the Black/White power scenario relative to the music industry. Although one cannot argue with the fact that White ownership of the industry still controls Black involvement, there is a certain cultural authority that is tied to Blackness here. Dre, as a businessman, recognizes the potential marketplace for a prominent White rapper. This is an ingenious idea because it understands the history around the White negro and the potential profit inherent. Yet when Black people appropriate, we often infuse this with negative connotations. Here, the idea of "pimpin" is juxtaposed against what with White people might be called appropriation. Can we see it the other way, though, or does power force us to see it as only a one-sided relationship?

In other words, it is easy as a society to see Blackness as being appropriated or being exploited because we have come to accept a certain victimization of Black culture to be an extension of the victim status that often is associated with Black people by liberal White assumptions. Yet, the question becomes, can we conceive of a landscape where Blackness can exploit and appropriate, and be seen as something other than reaffirming a stereotype and instead seen as empowerment? If a Black person appropriates Whiteness, he or she is seen as a sellout, yet when a White person appropriates Blackness, he or she is seen as cool.

White acceptance of and White participation in a Black form confers something like a legitimacy, and in a world defined by White supremacy, this sort of hegemonic relationship is almost endemic to the production of culture. When, though, if ever, will we be able to envision a situation where Black acceptance of and Black participation in a White form confers equal authority? When this comes, then it will be apparent to all that the playing field is no longer unbalanced but level across the board.

Epilogue

Where's the Love?

I don't want much/fuck I drove every car/some nice cooked food/some nice clean draws/bird ass niggas I don't mean to ruffle y'all/I know you're waitin' in wings/but I'm doin' my thing.

—Jay-Z, "Heart of the City"

Words are more powerful than fists.

—Muhammad Ali, on *The Mike Douglas Show*, July 17, 1974

I can remember vividly the first time I heard "Rapper's Delight" by the Sugarhill Gang. A couple of my boys had come by to scoop me up and when I got in that 1977 Ford Granada that day, all they could talk about was this new song they had heard on the radio. The problem was they couldn't really describe the tune. They didn't know the name of the song, nor did they know who it was by. They just kept saying that it was different, that it was like *talkin' over some beats*. They had heard it a few times on the radio, and assured me that it would come on again. As a matter of fact, we rode around that day until it eventually came on the radio.

I can hear it now, "What you hear is not a test/I'm rappin' to the beat . . ." As the song moved through each verse, from Wonder Mike, Big Bank Hank, and Master Gee, the momentum built to an incredible crescendo. Remember, this is 1979, back in the day, before all the radio stations were these corporate conglomerates with no unique identity that played the same shit repeatedly in a predictable fashion. No, this was when they played the extended version of "Rapper's Delight," all seven or eight minutes of it. I really liked the last verse on that extended version, "[H]ave you ever gone over to a friend's house to eat/and the food just ain't no good?/I mean the macaroni's soggy/the beans all mushed/and the chicken taste like wood." That was the shit!

"Rapper's Delight" was like a bolt of lightning for me. Everyone else I knew had been listening to Michael Jackson's *Off the Wall* album as if it were the last record they would ever hear. Now, that record was cool, and it now seems even better, considering that it was the last album Michael made before completely losing his mind, but considering that so many other people were into it, I needed to have something else to listen to, something else to distinguish my musical taste from the masses. "Rapper's Delight" would serve that purpose and it would open a door into a culture and a worldview that would still continue to inform me, even today.

I was committed to learning every word in every verse of that song. We even had a contest to see who could recite the whole song from memory. I won that contest going away. It got to the point where cats would come to me in the lunchroom and ask me to rap it for them, and I gladly obliged. A short time thereafter I heard Kurtis Blow do "Christmas Rappin" and it was on, again. I loved this new rap thing, better than a hog loved slop!

Language has always been fascinating to me. This is why rap appealed to me so much. It was a new language. It drew on the style that I had heard growing up, all around me. From the preacher's rap to the disc jockey's rap on the radio, to the niggas on the corner who would use these clever rhymes as a way of identifying themselves. I remember once when I was real young and I got a new tape recorder for Christmas that year, and I was going around taping whatever I could. This nigga down the street, Eddie Bullock, asked me to let him say something on the recorder. I hesitated, and told him not to say no shit that would get me in trouble with Mom Dukes, and he agreed not to. Of course, when he got the mic in his hand, he went off, signifying and "playing the dozens."

Though I wanted to stop him, some magnetic force held me back. I was momentarily frozen in my steps. He was mesmerizing. Though I knew I had to erase this before Mom Dukes heard it, and I was pissed that he had done just what I asked him not to do, I couldn't help myself. I listened to this over and over again. It was so transgressive, so vulgar, and I loved it.

I was impressed by both the rhyming style and the fact that Eddie seemed to be waiting for the opportunity to say this. He had a huge grin on his face when he let out his words. See, Eddie was one of these cats, like a lot of other Brothas, who the school system had decided was "retarded" and he was isolated in this segregated world known as "Special Ed," so he didn't really socialize with the rest of us too much, though we all knew him. Well, on that day, Eddie might have been deemed "retarded" by the mainstream White establishment, here represented by the school system, but to me, he was a wordsmith of the highest order.

The power of the word has always impressed me, especially, I must admit, its transgressive qualities. Though as a child I was surrounded by many Black people, Black men in particular, who had no control of their lives in the outside world, who were truly unfulfilled in their quest for self empowerment, who had no agency whatsoever but who had absolute command of the words that came out of their mouths. It made no difference what kind of inferior posture they had to assume on a daily basis, what kind of shit they had to take from the "White man," they had complete control of their words, their conversation. Again, this ranged from the many "jackleg" preachers I had heard to the coldest pimps you ever wanted to meet. Language was their thing, no doubt.

A short time after I immersed myself in this evolving rap thing, I heard Gil Scot-Heron for the first time. Shortly after the election of Ronald Reagan, I heard Scot-Heron's tune "B Movie," which was an engaged critique of the direction the country was moving after the election of such a right-wing figure as Reagan. Man, that song still rings in my head today. Though I was only sixteen and not yet legal to vote, Scot-Heron's words turned me into an impassioned Reagan-hater. Now, many people would not consider Gil Scot-Heron hip hop because of his age, but his ability to weave sly metaphor with political analysis, and still rhyme tight, was incredible, and very much formative relative to what would become hip hop. I was especially fond of the way he listed the warmongers who dotted Reagan's first cabinet: George "Papa Doc" Bush, Casper "The Defensive" Weinberger, and "Atilla the Haig." Scot-Heron's point that Reagan's highest accomplishment in Hollywood was playing second to the monkey Bonzo was not lost on me. I began to get deeper and deeper into politics at that time, studying the cabinet, scrutinizing Reagan's "voodoo economics," and counting the days until this clown would no longer be in office. Well, of course, I was counting for a long time.

> A child is born with no state of mind/blind to the ways of mankind/God is smilin' on you/but he's frownin' too/cause only God knows what you'll go through.
>
> —Grand Master Flash and the Furious Five,
> featuring Melle Mel, "The Message"

All of this came to a head during my first semester in college, in the summer of 1982 at the University of Florida. Some cats who hailed from the infamous "Bucktown" (Overtown) section of Miami and who lived downstairs from me in the dorm had taken their financial aid money and purchased a new stereo, and they had a gang of albums to boot. They kept playing this twelve-inch record by Grand Master Flash and the Furious Five, featuring Melle Mel. That shit was so dope! Of course, the record I'm referring to is "The Message," one of the most important songs ever made.

"The Message" was a muthafucka, it combined the dopest rhymes with a most astute level of political commentary on the effect Reagan's policies were having on the Black community. I couldn't stop listening to "The Message." Again, everybody else was listening to Michael Jackson's *Thriller* album and watching his groundbreaking videos by now, and so I really needed another outlet. I had grown to hate Michael, who was trying to look more and more like a White person with every passing day. The fact that so many people across campus, Black, White, male, female, were listening to the same thing made me nervous.

Though I did not grow up in New York, I have been a fan of hip hop ever since it made its way out of the Five Boroughs. I have been listening ever since. What I find so compelling is the way in which this relatively simple form of communication, rhymes over beats, however you slice it, is truly quite complex. Because Black people have always had to make do with so little, the relative abundance of one's own words is at times all we have to use in fighting against a corrupt and vicious society.

This is why hip hop is so important, and why it speaks to so many. It is at once humorous *and* a weapon of guerilla warfare against the sophisticated technology of the dominant order. Hip hop speaks in a code that allows people to communicate with one another beyond the eavesdropping that those in power often engage in. Like a lyrical tower of Babel, hip hop's confounding influence has at times had an ominous affect on society. For those who identify themselves with the mainstream, be they Black, White, or otherwise, hip hop is a pariah, something you want to get rid of because it attempts to tell the truth, in spite of the consequences that might accompany the telling of this truth.

When Chris Rock engages the hip hop practice of keepin' it real, he is tearing down the walls of secrecy that for too long have stifled the Black expressive tradition. It makes no difference who hears it, it needs to be said, and it needs to be said by someone who clearly has the best interests of his people at heart, however acerbic or caustic it might be otherwise. There is an attempt at honesty here that supersedes moral convention or racial protocol.

The very fact that hip hop continues to look for that which is real, in a world that can be so fake otherwise, is again a testament to hip hop's enduring significance. It is the desire to uncover the real, however elusive this quest might be, that makes hip hop such a worthwhile enterprise. While the debates in hip hop about who's real and who's not might be redundant on occasion, it reflects a larger interest in finding something substantive, deciphering some meaning in life that can far too often seem a waste of time.

It takes money to live in America, and it takes a lot of money if you want anything beyond the bare minimum. In spite of whatever struggles Black people have encountered in this society, the struggle to live a decent life is one that never subsides, no matter how much money you get.

When Danny Glover, a well-known actor made famous by the immense popularity of a franchise like the *Lethal Weapon* films, cannot get a cab in New York City, there is something seriously wrong. It's not that Glover is hard to recognize either. Do you realize how many people have seen those *Lethal Weapon* films? I bet Mel Gibson never got passed up by a cab before!

What is even more ironic is that for all those cabdrivers who would pass up Danny Glover, those same people would, more than likely, still want his autograph. This is the dilemma of being Black in America. You're at once loved for your unique contribution to society and simultaneously hated for being who you are. This irreconcilable difference is the push and pull that makes life nearly impossible to navigate. As Jay-Z says, "Can I live?"

Woke Up This Mornin' and Got Myself a Gun

In my mind, the pursuit of money, capital, cheese, paper, scrilla, fetti, and cake is a time-honored tradition in American culture. We have tended to praise those individuals who have pursued this capital, especially those who have done so with a particular flair. Figures like Joe Kennedy, of old, started out selling bootleg liquor and went on to enshrine his family as American royalty, his hustlin' past neatly erased from the picture. Or, look at America's continued fascination with mobsters, from Lucky Luciano to Meyer Lansky, from Don Corleone to, most recently, Tony Soprano. In each case, there was and remains a fascination with these individuals, their flamboyant lifestyle, and their penchant for drama. If we pay attention to the most recent case here, the overwhelmingly popular HBO program, *The Sopranos,* we can see this trend anew.

The Sopranos features an intimate portrayal of your typical suburban New Jersey family; the father, Tony; the mother, Carmela; their daughter, Meadow, who is a student at Columbia University; and their at times wayward young son, Anthony Jr. There is also the representation of an extended family that includes Tony's now-deceased mother, his conniving sister, and his Uncle Jr. The representation of their world is not unlike most other images of the suburban family, with the exception that the head of the household, Tony, is a mob boss. Now, *The Sopranos* is a wonderful television offering, no doubt. Its refreshing take on the suburban ideal is quite enjoyable and often enlightening as a form of popular culture.

Yet, can we imagine a similar program on, say, a Black drug kingpin? A program where the Black criminal figure is afforded a family and shown to practice his craft, while being able to skirt the law and remain viable, so as to further our investigation into the ironic nuances of daily family life? Not only is this something we cannot imagine, we know it would never exist. Even if by some strange stretch of the imagination it did, the connotations would still be drastically different.

No one, Black, White, or otherwise, is interested in the motivation of a Black drug dealer. No one wants to sympathize with a figure like this. No one assumes that a person like this deserves anything other than the penitentiary or death. This is an unevolved figure who is dehumanized from the jump. It is a figure that deserves no consideration whatsoever beyond consideration of shackles on his feet or a bullet in his muthafuckin' head!

> I Vito/voice of the young people/a mouthpiece for hustlers/I'm back muthafuckas!
>
> —Jay-Z, "The Ruler's Back"

Well, there are elements of hip hop that function very much like the Black version of *The Sopranos*. In this case, the intricate nuances of the life of a Black gangsta, through the voice of hip hop, gets the same sort of treatment and regard as that of the fictional Tony Soprano. If the culture can fictionalize the life of a White mobster, be it a truly fictional one like Tony, or a real-life figure like John Gotti, why can't the same be accorded a hip hop artist who uses the medium to articulate his or her life in streets? Why is it that when a Black artist filters and interprets his or her culture through a fictional medium, it is assumed to be literal. Again, hip hop is about the real, not the literal. It is about using a stylistic mode of address known as realism to render the speakers' lives for their listeners.

Hip hop artists are charged with articulating what they see, and the best of them do it with the same precision, the same distinct approach, as any great writer of fiction would. Hip hop is an art form, and like any art form, it, of course, is rooted in some sense of reality, for it must draw its impetus from somewhere. Yet so many want to read it literally, as though a rapper is actually cocking the trigger of a gun, while spittin' sixteen bars in the studio.

During the summer of 2001, the young actor Robert Iler, who plays Anthony Jr. on *The Sopranos* was arrested in New York on charges of assault, robbery, and smoking weed, with a *posse* of other individuals. Iler's actions seem to parallel the actions of the mischievous character he plays on the show, but will there be a public outcry that suggests that Iler is a thug and that because of this the show should be taken off the air? Not likely. Though some lone individuals have expressed that the show demeans Italian Americans, this in no way stands the chance of becoming a national outrage or cause for censorship from some avaricious politicians. The reason being is that we too often in this country use the actions of wayward White people as simply the actions of individuals, yet we often take the actions of one Black person and use them to represent an entire race of people. For this reason, in the wake of the Robert Iler arrest, we do not have to worry about the profiling by police of young White actors in the way that they have clearly profiled rappers and young Black men in general.

The point is, many young White men now routinely embrace Black culture as a way of defining and making distinct their particular brand of masculinity. One need only look to a film like Ben Younger's *Boiler Room* (2000), in which the main character played by Giovanni Ribisi begins the film directly quoting from the legendary Biggie Smalls cut "Things Done Changed" at the outset of the narrative; it is used as a verbal epigraph that sets in motion the tale of White male greed run amok in the world of finance. Ribisi even states that the stock market is the White man's version of selling crack, further aligning Whiteness with this societally accepted version of Black masculinity and by extension, hip hop.

For many years some people have suggested that Black people sell dope because they are denied the opportunities to make a living in the legitimate world, but *Boiler Room* turns this around and uses the example of the wealthy, calculated, and efficient Black drug dealer, as told through many hip hop scenarios, as a model for capitalist excellence.

Not only is White masculinity interested in appropriating perceived Blackness in terms of dope dealing and money management though, one can also see this in other aspects of the culture as well. For instance, the number of White men now, many of them legitimate corporate citizens, who don a bald head and a goatee, while embracing one another with a handclasp and hug, "showin' love," as it were, in the style made famous by so many hip hop figures and otherwise visible Black men in general.

The appropriation is also evident in another example that foregrounds the influence that Black thought has had on our former president and newly appointed prime minister of Harlem, Slick Willie, himself. Speaking to students at his alma mater Georgetown University on November 7, 2001, about the events of September 11, Clinton took a somewhat different tack than the overwhelming mood of patriotic fervor that engulfed America in the aftermath of these events.

The former president, whose words were reported in a November 8, 2001, article appearing in the conservative *Washington Times* says that "here in the United States, we were founded as a nation that practiced slavery, and slaves quite frequently were killed even though they were innocent." He goes on to say that "this country once looked the other way when a significant number of native Americans were dispossessed and killed to get their land or their mineral rights or because they were thought of as less than fully human." Clinton added that "we are still paying a price today."

Though these comments were curiously not given much national press coverage, the way in which Clinton seized the opportunity to detail the events in a much broader light than had been the case previously is interesting. Clinton broke ranks with the almost obligatory tone of patriotic rhetoric that emerged in the immediate aftermath of the events by making bold statements that went counter to the "America as victim" sentiment, which seemed to define the consensus public mood.

What was also interesting, though, was that Clinton drew on the logic of Malcolm X in making his claims. It was Malcolm who many years previously, went against public sentiment and stated that the assassination of John F. Kennedy was a result of "chickens coming home to roost," in relation to the fact that Kennedy's death was not an isolated incident but one in a series of prolonged moments, and simply one that enacted its vengeance on an American figure.

Clinton's comments were not widely reported, but they did carry the same sentiment forward, recognizing that both slavery and the annexation of Native American land were acts of terror, though seldom regarded as such. The point here is that the lingering influence of Malcolm's ideas have been absorbed by a former president, a former president whose close connection to Black culture demonstrates the viability of this culture in a most visible fashion. Yet, in this case, it is not that Black culture needed Bill Clinton, but it is the fact that Bill Clinton needed Black culture.

Clinton's appropriation of Black style is what made him stand out as a large and powerful public figure seemingly down for the cause, and, more important, down for Black people. However specious this connection may actually be is somewhat secondary to what appearances suggest here. When Clinton clothes himself in Blackness, he gives an endorsement at the highest level of American authority, and in doing so, he attests the prevailing significance of the culture in no uncertain terms. It is as though the strength of the culture is such that he cannot help but be informed by it.

Maybe this is why so many have tried desperately to keep the races separated for so long—because it was known that once Blackness got out in the open its ability to influence would operate unfettered? Once you go Black, you never go back. It is not lost in all of this that hip hop was the prevailing form of Black expression during the time that Clinton chose to represent and that hip hop itself flourished during this same time.

At the end of the day we live in a society where culture assumes a very prominent role. It was such in the 1960s that the civil rights movement became a culture of sorts, a culture with its own music, its own images, its own way of being. This culture was in subsequent years repackaged and injected into our collective memory via imagery. I often point to the groundbreaking Blackside documentary series *Eyes on the Prize* which was originally broadcast on PBS during the late 1980s as a perfect example of how the era of the civil rights movement will be remembered. PBS has come to assume a prominent place in the retelling of various aspects of the American historical narrative, and this being the case, *Eyes on the Prize* serves as the representation of record, if you will, when it comes to visualizing civil rights. In addition, Hollywood has now consistently produced films that are set during the civil rights era and almost suggest that racism and its attendant difficulties are a thing of the past, safe to be relegated to a history far removed from contemporary culture. It is as though racism is historical and not contemporary.

The fact that the events of the civil rights era lend themselves so well to being represented visually has made it so that society as a whole uses these visual images—what I like to refer to as "dogs and waterhoses"—to forever define how race and racism function. Yet, in the aftermath of this perfectly visual time, contemporary race and its subtle and nuanced functions often get dismissed, for it is now routinely assumed that in order for racism to exist it must live up to these lofty standards set by the spectacular visual images of the past.

The other lingering remnant of civil rights lies in the way that we now assume that this era defined Blackness for the ages, that in order to be truly Black, one had to have been attacked by dogs and doused with waterhoses, that one had to be forced to get up from a segregated lunch counter in order to claim to be truly Black. In all of this, Blackness was cloaked in suffering and defined by the degree to which one had been abused.

My point is not to make light of this but, instead, to point out the limited nature of continually pursuing such a dead-end street. If Blackness can be defended only as suffering, then what was the point of pursuing a free and open society? What was the point of trying to knock down the walls that denied Black people the opportunity for advancement when all we were going to do was erect new walls that contained our progress, and made that progress hostage to the struggles that attempted to make advancement possible in the first place?

The civil rights movement was dour, it was serious, and it was ultimately heavy in the way that it bore on the soul. Many people, Black, White, and otherwise, have embraced this era while rejecting any subsequent era as failing to live up to the standards of the one previous. It is within their best interest to hold civil rights up as the "be-all-end-all" of race in America. This is not only self-serving, it is utterly regressive.

America has now turned Martin Luther King Jr.'s dream into a long weekend. In other words, civil rights has passed; get over it!

Hip hop has not completely forgotten civil rights though. No, as a matter of fact, hip hop has done a great deal to firmly place the moments of this era in a larger historical context. The music and culture have always attempted to remember the past, yet have also urged us to move forward.

What hip hop has done is taught us that true freedom and liberation can begin only if we move beyond being concerned about doing things the "right" way. Hip hop continually embraces contradiction as opposed to trying to make everything seem perfect, trying to make everything conform to a dominant moral idea.

At this point, one cannot even begin to discuss American culture without dealing with Black culture, and this continues to increase with each passing day. Recognizing this cultural impact, hip hop then, in my mind, is ultimately the model that best allows us to understand the present generation of African Americans, and by extension, the present generation of Americans. This culture allows us to understand how the present generation is so very different from previous generations of Black people, for the present generation has grown up at a different time in history.

Hip hop also allows us to begin to understand how this generation might make sense of their future, which will most certainly be different from the way that previous generations have reconciled their issues. In addition, hip hop is a prominent vehicle for expression, for culture has been one of the more visible areas of society where Blacks have consistently had the most representation.

My words are not intended as a diss of civil rights. No. It is amazingly obvious what a profound effect that moment in history has had on the world, and it certainly hit home in America. Civil rights will forever be an integral part of the American master narrative.

Yes, it is unfortunate that many people's lives were lost fighting in this struggle. Yes, it is quite unfortunate also that people had to fight for this in the first place. Blood was shed, no doubt. It is also not as though I'm saying that racism has disappeared today either. By no means has it disappeared. I am not even saying that it has subsided, though it has, like the times themselves, been altered to fit a new age.

What I am saying is that we cannot live in the past forever. Civil rights had its day; now it is time to move out of the way. Civil rights was a struggle, and it remains an ongoing struggle for all disenfranchised people of color to pursue their civil rights. But many in the civil rights era have for too long gloated in a sanctimonious fashion, assuming that their day would never come to an end. This arrogant posture did little to inspire a new generation but went a long way toward alienating them. The posture of civil rights was such that it made future generations uncomfortable having to wear such restraints as they attempted to represent themselves.

Hip hop has allowed them to throw off those shackles, and though it is far from prefect, it does attempt to navigate the world in a very different way. Having survived the naysayers who from the beginning said that hip hop was only a musical trend, the culture, some twenty-plus years later, represents something far beyond music even.

Hip hop is a lifestyle. It is an ideology. It is a mode of being. It is an all-encompassing life force that far supersedes any dismissive tactic from those whom Flava Flav once chided as "nonbelievers." No matter how much you want to dismiss it, it is still here, having passed many tests, and poised to triumph even more in the future.

Hip hop is a testament to overcoming the obstacles that American life often imposes on its Black and Latino subjects, and in this, it is a model of what "we shall overcome" means in the modern world. To quote someone who, were he alive today, would most certainly find his voice in hip hop, William Shakespeare: hip hop, maybe more than any other contemporary form, truly embodies "the sweet uses of adversity/which, like the toad ugly and venomous/wears yet a precious jewel in his head."

Selected Bibliography

Aubrey, Erin. "Back Is Beautiful: Does the Public's Embrace of Jennifer Lopez's Abundant Butt Signal a Cultural Revolution or Simply the Triumph of Watered Down Multiculturalism?" Salon.com. July 15, 1998.

Boyd, Todd. "A Nod to Cool or a New Blaxploitation." *Los Angeles Times*. August 8, 1998. pp. 2, 17.

———. *Am I Black Enough for You? Popular Culture from the 'Hood and Beyond*. Indiana University Press. 1997.

Boyd, Todd (ed., with Kenneth Shropshire*). Basketball Jones: America above the Rim*. NYU Press. 2000.

Curl, Joseph. "Clinton Calls Terror a U.S. Debt to Past." *Washington Times*. November 8, 2001.

Dyson, Michael Eric. *Holler If You Hear Me: In Search of Tupac Shakur*. Basic Books. 2001.

———. *I May Not Get There with You: The True Martin Luther King Jr*. Free Press. 2000.

Etine, Jon. *Taboo: Why Black Athletes Dominate Sports and Why We're Afraid to Talk about It*. Public Affairs Press. 2000.

George, Nelson. *Hip Hop America*. Viking Press. 1998.

Hirschberg, Lynn. "How Black Comedy Got the Last Laugh." *New York Times Magazine*. September 3, 2000. p. 34.

Hoberman, John. *Darwin's Athletes: How Sport Has Damaged Black America and Preserved the Myth of Race*. Houghton Mifflin. 1997.

Jonnes, Jill. *Hep Cats, Narcs, and Pipe Dreams: A History of America's Romance with Illegal Drugs*. Johns Hopkins University Press. 1999.

MacAdams, Lewis. *Birth of the Cool: Beat, Be Bop, and the American Avant Garde*. Free Press. 2001.

Mailer, Norman. *Advertisements for Myself*. Harvard University Press. 1992.

Morrison, Toni. "The Talk of the Town." *New Yorker*. October 5, 1998. pp. 31–39.

Neal, Mark Anthony. *Soul Babies: Black Popular Culture, and the Post-Soul Aesthetic*. Routledge Press. 2001.

———. *What the Music Said*. Routledge Press. 1998.

Powell, Kevin (ed). *Step into a World: A Global Anthology of the New Black Literature*. John Wiley and Sons. 2000.

Price, S. L. "What Ever Happened to the White Athlete?" *Sports Illustrated*. December 8, 1997. pp.30–51.

Robinson, Randall. *The Debt: What America Owes to Blacks*. Plume Books. 2001.

Rose, Tricia. *Black Noise: Rap Music and Black Culture in Contemporary America*. University Press of New England. 1994.

Simmons, Russell, with Nelson George. *Life and Def: Sex, Drugs, Money, and God*. Crown Books. 2001.

Vincent, Ricky. *Funk: The Music, the People, and the Rhythm of the One*. St. Martin's Press. 1996.

X, Malcolm, and Alex Haley. *The Autobiography of Malcolm X*. Grove Press. 1964.

Glossary of Hip Hop Terms

The ATL: Atlanta

baby mama drama: controversy surrounding parenthood

battle rap: a competitive hip hop song

be down: to be committed

beef: a disagreement, an argument

Bentley: a playa's car of choice

bitin': to imitate, to copy

bling bling: possessing abundant jewelry, the brilliant sparkle of a diamond

blow up the spot: to take over, to bring attention to

bring it on: go ahead and do it

brothas: Black men

Bucktown: ghetto section of Miami, Florida

cake: money

capped: to get shot

cappin': to engage in a competitive game of verbal wordplay, the dozens

cat: a man, dude

cheese: money

chitlin': historical Black vaudeville circuit

Chocolate City: urban city centers with a major Black population, Washington, D.C.

choppin' up game: to explain a situation

Chronic: highly potent marijuana

clowned: (*to get clowned*): to be ridiculed

come up: to succeed; (*came up*): achieved success

coonin': to engage in stereotypical behavior

crunk: to get things going, to bring energy to a situation

cut: a song, also a track

The D: Detroit

the dirty South: the southern United States

dissin': to disrespect

dope connect: a drug connection, dealer

down for the cause: committed to political action

down for whatever: committed to flexibility

dropped: released to the public

droppin' some knowledge: articulating meaningful information

drops an intellectual bomb: to say something of immense significance

fetti: money

flips the script: to change

flossin': to show off, to flaunt

flow: verbal articulation; one's rap style

fo shizzle my nizzle: "for sure my nigga," hip hop slang

from the jump: from the beginning, at the outset

fronts: to give a false representation; also gold or platinum jewelry placed over the teeth, as in "gold fronts"

the game: life, a particular walk of life

gators: alligator shoes

gettin' money: to aggressively make money

ghetto fabulous: Black style in excess

get into my groove: to do things my way

having love: to respect

hate, *to hate on*: to hate, *the haters*: jealous, envious people; enemies; see playa-hatin'

hip hop culture: the music, clothes, lifestyle, and politics of hip hop

hip hop heads: true hip hop fans; aficionados

homies: friends, comrades

ice: diamonds

irregardless: black modification of "regardless," to the second degree

illest: the best, the top,

jackleg: an amateur

jeffin': see coonin'

keepin' it real: honesty, to be honest despite consequences

mad lyrical skills: the ability to rap with great precision

MC: microphone controller

mo' money mo' problems: the more money you get, the more problems you accumulate

mozzarella: money

muthafucka: modern spelling and pronunciation of "motherfucker," meaning may vary from positive to negative, according to context

nigga: modern hip hop appropriation, spelling of "nigger"

old school: traditional, old fashioned

on point: to be correct

on some new shit: a new way of thinking

on some other shit: to be a nonconventional thinker

paper: money

phat: empowered

pimped: stylish; pimped out: highly accessorized

playa: a hip, stylish individual

playa-hatin': jealousy, envy

the playas ball: annual gathering and award show for pimps

props: to acknowledge, recognize

punk: a weak person

R&B: rhythm and blues, "rap-n-bull-shit"

rep: to represent

representin': to be representative of

rocked the house: to excite an audience

rocks: to sound good; also crack cocaine

rollin': driving or riding

the scene: the place, environment of a situation

scoop, scoop me up: to pick up

scrilla: money

sell-out: to compromise for money or social acceptance

shinin': to show off, like flossin'

signifyin': see cappin'

sucking on that glass dick: smoking crack cocaine

spittin' rhymes: to rap

spittin' sixteen bars: rhyming in standard hip hop song format

squab: to fight, to squabble

my steez: my style

street credibility: to be accepted as valid

thug life: the ethos and lifestyle of a thug, made famous by Tupac

tight verse: a particularly nice lyric

track: a song, or the street where a prostitute displays herself

tricking off: to adorn

true heads: see hip hop heads

underground: nonmainstream

vine: a suit

wack: terrible, sad, dismissable

walk the track: to put on display

whip: a car

the wrong nigga to fuck wit': the wrong person to bother

Shout Outs

Yes yes y'all. Once again it's on. Time to show love to those who in one way or another offered support, inspiration, and assistance in helping me finish another book.

Peace to Ed Boyd, the man who put the 'g' in game, and who taught me how to stand strong and stand firm on this thing of ours. Peace to Mozelle Boyd, who took me to my first concert as a reward for good grades, back in the day: Barry White and The Ohio Players at Olympia Stadium. Fo sho! Peace to the two of you for keeping the crib stocked with great music and provocative reading material, and thanks so much for subscribing to magazines other than *Ebony* and *Jet*.

Peace to Sonja Steptoe for all the love and all the laughs. Ain't no love in the heart of the city, but there's much love in the heart of Sonja. Your support is invaluable. Be ever wonderful.

Peace to my dawgs: Patrick "Jatty" Smith, Rick "The Ruler" Famuyiwa, David Was, Robert Hurst, Carl "Live Music" Fletcher, Javier "5" Jimenez, Larry Platt, and James "FM Backwards" Scott. Real niggas do real things!

A special shout out to my East Coast dawg Ken Shropshire, representin' the Iledelph. Peace to the coolest muthafucka alive, Gil Friesen, and to my Swedish homie, Jan Olsson, representin' over in Stockholm. Game recognize game. No doubt!

Peace to my 'SC crew, Emily Lacy, my nigga Jihad, Elizabeth Ramsey, Sherall Preyer, Raqi Syed, O. Thaddeus Frazier, and Kerry Perdue. Your invaluable assistance has made it possible for me to stay focused on my gig, knowing that you had my back. Good lookin'.

Peace to Eric Zinner for recognizin' the skills and for not sweatin' the technique. Peace to Michael Dear at the SC 2 Center for funding much of the research that went into this book and for your sponsorship of the Hip Hop 2000 conference. Peace to all the true hip hop heads out there representin' on the critical tip, especially Michael Eric Dyson, Mark Anthony Neal, and all others who truly know the steez.

Peace to all the prophets of rage, Big Willes, real niggas, b boys, b girls, and young Black entrepreneurs, who are out there gettin' money, politickin', and constantly giving me something to write about.

Finally, I say peace to all the playa haters, both past and present, who have provided me with much motivation by tryin' to stop my flow, tryin' to put salt in my game, and tryin' to stagnate my process.

This is number-four baby, and I ain't even in the groove yet. Damn, he's on TV again!

Peace

Index

About the Author

A frequent media commentator, Todd Boyd is a professor of Critical Studies in the USC School of Cinema-Television. His books include *Am I Black Enough For You? Popular Culture from the 'Hood and Beyond* and, as co-editor, *Basketball Jones: America above the Rim*, available from NYU Press. He produced and cowrote the Paramount Pictures film *The Wood*.